A Bite-Sized Business Book

The Average Wage Millionaire

Can *Anyone* Really Get Rich?

Art Rain

Published by Bite-Sized Books Ltd 2018

Although the publisher and author have used reasonable care in preparing this book, the information it contains is distributed as is and without warranties of any kind. This book is not intended as legal, financial, social or technical advice and not all recommendations may be suitable for your situation. Professional advisers should be consulted as needed. Neither the publisher nor the author shall be liable for any costs, expenses or damages resulting from use of or reliance on the information contained in this book.

©Art Rain 2018

Bite-Sized Books Ltd Cleeve Croft, Cleeve Road, Goring RG8 9BJ UK
information@bite-sizedbooks.com
Registered in the UK. Company Registration No: 9395379

The right of Art Rain to be identified as the author of this work has been asserted by him in accordance with the Copyright, Design and Patents Act 1988

ISBN: 9781720259701

Published by:

Bite-Sized Books Ltd
Cleeve Croft, Cleeve Road, Goring RG8 9BJ UK
information@bite-sizedbooks.com
Registered in the UK. Company Registration No: 9395379

To Ali & Viki

One who is cash rich (mostly with our money) but fritters away her time, the other who suspects she could do better with her money, but has no time!

Author – Art Rain

Art has had real jobs before he started writing, including giving financial advice!

In the 80s he was a fully certified Banker, providing HSBC clients with loans and savings advice. He ethically sold the first really large mortgage protection policy in the Midlands (years before PPI miss-selling claims dogged the industry) and tried to provide honest unbiased help to his clients, notwithstanding the anomaly that even senior staff in banks often earnt little more than the UK minimum wage themselves!

With a faultless lending record, Art took a surprising change in direction (and pay cut) to quit retail banking to follow his ambitions in marketing, joining a leading card issuer. Perhaps unsurprisingly he's never paid a penny in interest but he was interested in online innovation so jumped into the bank's Idea Incubation Lab before quitting to raise venture capital (as it was risky) and start his own business.

So that's two strong clues already to some of the important themes in this book, one about interest the other about risk and money!

After a business exit with his business partner in 2010 selling out to a PLC, Art started a boutique online marketing agency called Seriously Helpful and alongside running a small property portfolio, he tries to be seriously helpful to clients again.

He's a bit OCD with data so unlike many celebrity money management books written with either the benefit of hindsight or through rose tinted spectacles, Art has had access to a unique treasure trove of 40+ years of personal financial records enabling him to reconstruct almost exactly how his family have made their money, and wasted it too, all with some very surprising conclusions as a result. He genuinely did not know the ending of the story or the book when he first put pen to paper.

It's a journey starting from below average wage through to driving an Aston Martin, owning a small property portfolio and several business interests putting the family in the top 0.25% of the UK's wealthy as multi-millionaires. Yet the family are grounded and you're more likely to see them in Aldi than Waitrose or Harrods. Like many investors, they're not cash rich and assets are invested, that's how they became wealthy. Or is it? You'll have to read on to see if there is more to the story.

Paul Davies Bite-Sized Books Limited

Important Wealth Warning

This book is a record of one family's experiences of money over four decades and how it gets used and abused, often unintentionally. I hope it provides strong clues and real life lessons for others to think about when learning about money themselves but it should not be seen as financial advice or a route-map to simply slavishly follow.

This is because times change and everyone's circumstances and start point are a little different. Most importantly is the fact that I am no longer recognised as a qualified financial advisor, not because I was disqualified or anything like that, I simply don't work in that sector now so haven't kept on sitting the regular tests and exams – but I did pass them all in the early days and had a particularly good record inside the Bank.

For professional advice you should always seek out a current UK Independent Financial Advisor (IFA) or a comparable expert if you are an international reader and then listen carefully to what they say. But please don't be afraid to ask a few difficult questions based on experiences learnt in this book or elsewhere, and as the book shows, it's not always a bad idea to use your own judgement and intuition too.

Don't forget that advisors may be on commission, so be careful at all times where your money is concerned as you can be sure as eggs are eggs that everyone is after a little bit of it!

Contents
Important Wealth Warning
Letter from the Author
      Introduction
Chapter 1
      Is our story interesting?
Chapter 2
      It nearly didn't happen
Chapter 3
      Have we achieved the impossible?
Chapter 4
      What's that in Real Money?
Chapter 5
      Einstein and the Power of Compounding
Chapter 6
      Reference Tables
      1: Doing Nothing vs Earning or Paying Interest
      2/3 : Past Inflation & Investment Calculations
      4/5 : Forward Inflation & Investment Calculations
Chapter 7
      How many Accounts?!
Chapter 8
      And what about Mortgages?
Chapter 9
      In pictures too
Chapter 10
      APR's and Confusing Stuff.
Chapter 11
      Arbitrage & Cakes
Chapter 12
      How Did We Spend and Make Money?.
      Where We Invested

Chapter 13
>Let's Break Down the Investments in More Detail

Chapter 14
>SAYE, National Savings, Day Trading, Hot Tips, Profit Sharing, Bonds

Chapter 15
>Houses and Cars

Chapter 16
>Other ways to save money

Chapter 17
>Day to Day Purchases

Chapter 18
>Keeping Stuff a long time

Chapter19
>Refunds

Chapter 20
>Where has the wealth ended up?

Chapter 21
>Would I do it like this again?

Chapter 22
>Risk

Footnote

Summary

Appendix of useful links

Bite-Sized Business Books

Bite-Sized Books Catalogue

Letter from the Author

I was expecting this book, my eighth, to be a breeze to write, as I literally had at my fingertips almost 40 years of records on which to base my research. It turned out to be anything but a breeze as whilst the facts emerged relatively easily, lets face it, even if you like money it can be a bit of a dry topic. So the time was taken in trying to make this a story even people who don't like numbers can get to grips with. So you'll see that in each section I have provided either an early summary, fact or headline – so that's all you need to read if you are in a hurry or bored, but if you are the kind of person who likes detail, you can read on for that too.

If you are really into your mathematics it won't take long to spot some irregularities in the numbers and this is due in part to the fact that statistics like averages can be misleading, I don't always have 100% of the data I would like (so have added in some government statistics for example) and that variances caused by our own circumstances are simply too complicated to explain in detail without making the book even more dry than needed! So apologies, the general trends and themes are what I wanted to try and explain, not accuracy to 1%.

I do hope the book doesn't come across as boastful in any way – it's hard to achieve that when discussing a taboo subject like money. We are nothing special, just a normal if slightly eccentric family with fairly typical habits but perhaps a greater than average passion for savings. I am impressed by what we have achieved for ourselves from a modest start point. I wouldn't dream of comparing what we have achieved with anyone else, rich or poor. I am merely benchmarking our success against the supposedly important milestone called millionaire as it seems the most generally recognised, whether in £ or $.

Its perhaps no surprise that one of the morals of this little story is to start saving what you can when you can – I think the real trick is to get yourself in the mindset that saving isn't a punishment on yourself, like say, dieting, in fact it's the opposite, a chance to consume more, but just at a different time and place. Its nothing more than a habit that anyone can adopt, even if you are on the average wage or less.

I have always been pretty hot on goal setting and I'm sure having a vision to retire (if I wanted to) at fifty, spurred on this habit when it was tempting to flag. Seeing redundancies every year in the workplace was another motivating factor!

What you then do with your habit is then of course key and I hope our story provides some inspiration and a few surprises you can check out more fully for yourself.

Art Rain, London August 2018

Introduction

This book's goal is to guide you through our life so you can see for yourself how it was possible to start on a below average wage, save a little, use the money wisely, and end up wealthy.

All kinds of lessons will be revealed for you to consider. Any one of these might help you or my daughter and her friend Ali make better decisions regarding what to do with your own hard won cash. I hope so any way.

My goal is to provide ammunition to reinforce the thought that being a saver isn't a punishment, its simply **delaying enjoyment** so you can spend **more** later. The book will share the kind of insights I liberally sprinkle on colleagues at work, for example, "It's better to invest in your own home than rent as by the time you retire you'll have paid your landlord £400,000 and won't have anything to downsize for your old age or to leave the kids."

I think if more people in the UK could grasp that sometimes it's better to invest than borrow and it's better to save than spend then our nation wouldn't be steeped in debt. Our pensioners would be better off than those in countries like Croatia and Turkey who are doing significantly better than us, and yet we're supposedly the "experts" with one of the world's top financial markets on our doorstep. Somethings going wrong somewhere.

So I hope you like the book at least as much as my daughter and her friend do and I hope too that you find it informative and that it helps as part of your own financial education journey, and let's face it, what a tortuous journey it can be as money touches so many aspects of our lives from childhood through to parenting and old age. It's important to do your best with what you have, whether that means living life to the full today (as who knows what lies around the corner) or preparing yourself and your descendants for possible rainy days ahead which can impact anyone, especially if you live to 110.

> **Editor's note** — You are being a bit optimistic there but UK life expectancy does seem on average to be heading ever closer to 90. Pensions are of course likely to keep getting squeezed and pushed ever further back (from the current anticipated age of 67), so that's a lot of years to plan for rainy days or ill health in old age when typically income is lower, at least in the UK.
>
> **Author's note** — you've stolen my thunder, without adequate savings isn't it just a ticking time bomb? How on earth can future generations survive on pensions which are amongst the worst in Europe? But more on that hot topic later!

So back to the plot, I hope you like the book and find it useful, and if you don't then blame Vici and Ali for setting me down this path in the first place.

> **Note for Editor** - Do I have the time to add a couple of footnotes here, even though it's not the time for footnotes? The first being that I have also written as you know a Bite Sized book about how it's possible to afford an **Aston Martin** on a modest income — but that book isn't simply a rebadged version of the stories and lessons talked about here! So for anyone wanting an Aston Martin that's a good start point!

Secondly, as you know, I've also written about how Amazon may well impact the earnings potential of everyone, especially our grandchildren and beyond. An excellent article just out in the Guardian (July 2018) regarding life in Seattle, Amazon's home – see link in the appendices, suggests I might be ahead of time suggesting that these big multinationals are indeed ruining many peoples futures. In that book I jokingly suggested Mr Bezos (Amazons founder) should relocate from the West Coast to East Coast USA or even the UK to prolong his life expectancy and see more of the fruits of his business efforts. Based on what you've just revealed about UK life expectancy, they should be headquartering here! Jeff might then live to 2053 or thereabouts and that's almost long enough, by my calculations anyway, to see the Earth renamed as planet Amazon!

Editor's note – No, we don't have time for distractions, so let's continue with the money story.

Chapter 1

Is Our Story Interesting?

Just because I worked in a Bank, (my wife worked in retail) doesn't mean by right we have any useful knowledge or even an interesting story to impart, I think that right needs to be earned and proven to you through the course of our story, but before then it's probably a good idea to set the scene a little so you have a better idea who you are dealing with!

So I will first share some facts that show we have indeed risen from near poverty and that many people reading this book shouldn't despair, as they may already be further up the ladder than we were when we started out on our financial journey. And remember too that money is made and spent over decades, so even if you are coming to this particular party late, it's never too late to pick up some ideas that could reap rich rewards later in your life, even if you start late.

In short, we hope our story might be inspirational as in theory at least many people could emulate something similar in terms of patterns of behaviour if not the exact replication of transactions.

So here are some curious facts for you to ponder on before reading ahead in the context of how did we end up millionaires if these facts are true:

- My career started out at well below the UK average wage and even for the few years at its peak was only circa 50% above it.
- In Retail, and being female, sadly my wife has always earned below the average wage and due to

time off to raise our daughter, with subsequent Part Time and Zero-Hours working, this contributed to mean that on average, combined, we have **never earned consistently more than the UK household average wage.**

Things have of course improved a bit since we made our modest fortune (with a small f) but we are not what I consider rich nor even on any radar in comparison to the likes of Richard Branson, Peter Jones or Simon Cowell, even though my Aston gets confused with the latter! These days I aim to pay myself a salary broadly in the same ball-park as our other employees as we all do similar hours. So its an OK wage, not a huge one and not enough to run the car!

In short, we are nothing unusual at all and many people in many jobs or professions earn a lot more, so **how then is the title of this book possible**?

- Our total post tax earnings from employment during the 40 or so years under study add up to just over £1m, in fact £1,030,000 to be precise plus we had two modest inheritances totalling £48,000 but split between 3 people. So that's a grand total of £1.080,000 in income, which seems a lot to me but actually isn't that much as surely a life is worth more than half a million each?

So this leads onto the first odd fact that hopefully provides some testimony as to my money skills:

Even if we excluded the money made from business/inheritances, our current total asset value exceeds every penny we've EVER earned even if we'd not spent a single penny of it. On anything, no expenditure on food, no clothes, no cars, no property for example.

Or to put it another way:

- If we'd taken even penny of income (after tax) and squirreled it away under the mattress, (and blagged our parents to provide free accommodation, food and pay all the costs associated of bringing up our daughter), we'd still have made less than we have achieved through my careful money management!

I know, It's strange, and seems impossible but I promise you it's true. Plus of course in reality we can add in the value of business ventures etc so overall we've not done so badly at all and in fact have **tripled what we've ever earned, even if we'd never spent a single penny**!

- As you'll probably agree all this seems impossible, then strange fact two is that against those aforementioned earnings then of course we do need to deduct living costs as nobody has given us any kind of handouts from the age of 21, or 16 in my wife's case. And whilst Mrs R does maintain I am tight with money, we haven't exactly lived by skip-diving all these years!

At first glance our total living costs over the period add up to an equally surprising £1.06m, and this covers all the usual costs like mortgages, food, energy, petrol, clothes, council tax, for example.

The eagle eyed readers amongst you will have made 2+2 already (or should it be 2-2?) and realised that this leaves us with just £0.02m surplus income (more accurately **£18,000**) on which we must have surely laid the foundations to build our subsequent wealth? (£1.08m minus £1.06m), so you'd probably agree that's not a lot based on over 40 years hard work? It works out at about only £0.50 per day each!

Well – here is the stranger fact.

In calculating and checking this figure to find out how much we'd saved over the years (as from the outset I concluded saving must at least be part of our story) this alleged surplus spare cash was a spectre, it simply didn't exist and just like most other normal families we too were also living right up to or even beyond our means!

What had happened in my initial calculations was that I hadn't taken out any money for things that whilst I might consider them as **luxuries**, any other sane person would generally have regarded them as normal living costs! So I'd not factored in things like buying books and CDs, DVDs, and film services like Netflix or Amazon Prime (we don't have Sky) nor the £20,000 we have cumulatively spent on holidays.

> **Editor's note** – I see you are not big holiday people as that's only around £10 per week saved up for holidays, that is £500 per year.
>
> **Author's note** – Correct – we've had a few years without holidays due to pressure of work and the fact our teenage daughter has had ME for over a decade but even when we do get away I target to spend just £100 per person per night, all in, including spending money and the odd drinkie poo! Maybe this is where the tight with money reputation comes from?

Assuming most readers are not hermits or on a restricted Amish lifestyle and agree that they too would include such things as part of their own normal living costs then we have a further **£64,000** of *entertainment* expenditure to be added onto our costs.

So, far from a surplus, we appear to have in fact spent £46,000 more than we have collectively earned in the 40 years being studied!

1. So you may be wondering (I was): How are we driving Aston Martins and buying property all over the place?
2. How have we managed to build any wealth at all if we didn't even have any initial seed money?
3. And why are we not up to our ears in debt instead?

Editor's note - It is a bit odd. And on this point particularly I've just done a quick tot up and if you were overspending circa £1,100 a year for over 40 years, then even if you'd borrowed at a cheap rate, say, by adding it onto the mortgage, then today it would still add up to a debt of over £355,000….. A long way from being even wealthy with a small W!

Author's note – Yes, in addition you may be surprised to hear we are pretty much **totally debt free and have been for almost two decades** (since our early 40s).

NB. We do actually have a couple of buy to let mortgages on interest only deals but the lenders hold assets to repay these separate from the properties themselves and assets used in any of our calculations, so they can technically be ignored as they are balanced out. It's all for tax efficiency reasons or something like that!

So that's why I wrote this book. It felt like if I could only unearth the hidden message there might be a useful story to share. I just had to piece it all together for you like a detective, and what an interesting if arduous task it has been!

Chapter 2

It nearly didn't happen!

Aside from posterity and the love of a good detective mystery, there was of course a bit more to the story behind the book. I actually set out to write it at the behest of my daughter and her old school friend Ali, or to be more accurately I **considered** writing it and then dismissed it as I thought: "What's interesting about a small businessman or ex-banker rambling on about finance, however well intentioned?" And even though I'm interested (to a degree) in money myself, let's face it, it's a pretty dry subject at best, so who would want to read my thoughts?

As an ex-Banker I did of course always have a reasonable handle on how much the family assets were worth in total, and as I'm a bit OCD I'd even got spreadsheets tracking back the money flows over decades, these being compiled from paper records. But you'll be relieved to hear I'd **never bothered to try and work out** (who would?) precisely **how much we'd ever earned or spent.** So even though I had a lot of the data needed to do the calculations I'd never really studied it that much, until now, for you.

> **Editor's note** – Funnily enough I have a friend who jots down every single penny spent in a little book, I've no idea what he does with the masses of information collected but he does still pay his mortgage in cash each month by taking it physically into the Building Society, much to their surprise as he has a professional job and everyone normal pays by standing order!

Author's note – I've come across that too. I know people who steadfastly record the price of every litre of fuel they've ever bought. Have you noticed that it's always in a little black book?

But once I'd realised the strange facts I've just shared with you, namely, how did our wealth exceed all our income and how had we ended up moderately well off if we've spent more than we've earned, then obviously there was the makings of a good yarn and there was no stopping me getting to the bottom of this weird mystery.

I decided if I can work out, not only for my own sanity, how we'd managed to end up with assets and no debts despite on paper at least never earning that much, it could be a useful lesson to share, particularly as whilst I may have a reputation for financial prudence, I'm no David Blaine or Paul Daniels, with money that is, not rabbits and hats!

So one minute the book idea was on, then it was dismissed as too boring a topic, only to be back on again once I'd realised that our wealth exceeded our income even if we'd never spent a penny of it, and I was even more intrigued that all this was true even if you excluded our subsequent success in business and with property investment.

So here we are – the book has happened and I am going to attempt to walk you through our story of how we've achieved the seemingly impossible banker's equivalent of turning water into wine!

As I mentioned in the introduction I have put either a brief summary of Fact at the start of each section and those interested can read on for more detail, if that doesn't alleviate the boredom of finance than just read as if you are a Peeping Tom getting to share all our secrets. Mrs R does say I have been pretty frank but I wanted the story to be as transparent as possible so you can decide for yourself whether it's really true and possible to replicate!

> **Editor again** – I've heard Mrs R say that she has always wondered if you had a secret money tree or printing press at the end of the garden!
>
> **Author's note** – Sadly not but I have wondered what kind of tree lies at the end of celebrity gardens? How often do we read of celebrities earning a fortune yet ending up bankrupt? I have even considered providing pragmatic money management tips for people of high net worth so they are confident of at least getting back what they put in! Don't you think it must be absolutely heart-breaking to have to start a career from scratch when you lose it all, sometimes through little fault of their own other than choosing over confident advisors?

So I decided to do a bit more digging (pun intended), not in the garden but through our financial archives to get to the bottom of this seemingly crazy story and that's when I realised that the real significance in our experiences lies in what we did with our savings and the investments we've made over the years, and working out what's worked best. Plus of course leading on to a few ideas for how you save money in the first place, so the book aims to cover as much of this as possible to give others inspiration.

Chapter 3
Have We achieved the Impossible?

Actually No, and aside from the earlier comments, let's call them **FACTS:**

FACT 1. *About trying to never pay interest on credit cards*

FACT 2. *using others people's money when it's risky*. (This is probably the first important lesson my research has revealed.)

FACT 3. Statistics about money can be easily misleading, intentionally or otherwise.

Let me explain. I said earlier that our total earned income, after tax, was around £1,030,000, or £1,078,000 after inheritances. Spread over almost 42 years that works out as an average **joint** income of £24,500 per year. And against this we had a total expenditure of £1,124,000 so that's an average expenditure per year of £26,700, or a **shortfall** of, on average, £1,100 per year if we factor in the inheritances. So statistically it appears we were living above our means, or were we?

The reality is slightly different and proves in this case, **unintentionally**, that statistics can be misleading. They can also be used **intentionally** by unscrupulous lenders to make unaffordable things like pay-day loans or luxury cars suddenly appear completely **sensible and affordable** for all, (completely legally I should add) but more on those topics later.

So back to our statistics – Upon more detailed analysis it turns out that in fact obviously my wife didn't work all the time, (at work that is, she's busy at home – I thought I'd better add that in just in case she reads this!) and when we set up my company I had a six year period on 45% lower salary to help the business survive and prosper. During these periods we managed to cut our outgoings by around 30% but plainly you can't cut everything, so we did have short periods of overspending. But the emphasis is on **short**.

Conversely, when we started doing better financially, despite being generally frugal, (Mrs R and the Editor would say mean!), it's inevitable to splash the cash a bit more liberally. So for me, in recent years, we increased expenditure say on luxuries like coffee and cakes at Dunelm on a Sunday afternoon, (yes, I know how to treat the Mrs), days out in the Aston Martin I acquired, and maybe even leaving the heating on a bit longer than needed in the autumn! This all messes with the averages.

So when I took all this into account and recalculated the statistics with better data I arrived at the following estimates of a more accurate **real position**:

> Average **joint** salary **after tax** per annum = **£36,000**
>
> Average Expenditure on necessities & "luxuries" (like Netflix) = **£26.700**
>
> **Approx. Surplus = £9,300 per annum**
>
> NB. A surplus isn't a real surplus as its needed to fund things like pensions, savings, meals out and anything else you can think of that's more fun than TV. The good news here is the recalculation has revealed we do indeed have a surplus to play with versus the previous £1,100 shortfall!

So from a theoretical water-into-wine scenario we have in fact achieved financial success by the much less impressive feat of squirrelling away some savings. But I've discovered this kind of habit was formed from an early start point, in fact right from joining the world of work. So that's another lesson.

FACT 4. *Start being smart with money ASAP. Today is better than tomorrow or next week, even if it's only £1 saved.*

So we saved over £9,000 pa from the start?

FACT 5. *No, fluctuations in savings means on average we put aside 20% of income*

£9,300 per annum would be a crazy 35% of income and who could afford that if simultaneously you are paying living costs etc? In practice after allowing for all the variations that I've mentioned we managed to save, or should I say, not spend, around £210,000 over a 42 year period which equated to around 20% of our joint income after tax.

So we actually "saved" only around £5,000 per annum or £100 per week between us across all these years, sometimes a bit more, for example, when we'd been in a house for a while, sometimes a bit less, say, when we bought a new car or were moving home or changing jobs.

Averages here may of course not mean much as a lot changes over 40 years.

Chapter 4

What's that in real money?

FACT 6. At today's prices our income would be £5.3K a month, our costs £4k

What's that in real money is a good question to answer early on as of course telling you an average joint salary in say 1997 plucked from an analysis of 40+ years history is pretty meaningless to compare to today. So if we re-rated that to allow for inflation it would look more like this:

- Average Joint Salary £36,000 equates to £64,100 in today's money, so that's about **£5,350 per month** after tax for most people in the UK now
- Average Expenditure £26,700 equates to £47,500 at today's money or £3,950 pm

NB. Ali or Victoria, or Dear Reader, you can now more directly compare these figures to your own situation today.

So we thought we had a shortfall of £1,400 per month in today's money but as I have said, the shortfall was a statistical anomaly and in practice we were making "savings" for things like pensions etc. That average of £100 a week quoted above, in today's money i.e. allowing for inflation, actually works out today at around saving £775 a month.

Fact 7. We have always typically increased our net worth in 4 out of every 5 months

My analysis has also shown that by being diligent and regular savers as often as possible **we increased our family**

net worth (If you recall I've been tracking this in a spreadsheet for years and years) **in four out of every five months**, consistently across the 40 or so years studied. In short, saving became a **habit** not an exceptional event. Even allowing for periods of excess spending, e.g. when moving home, on average we still managed to typically save over £250 a month, but not always.

If you are interested in how it worked for us through the ages, even on low wages:

>Mid 1970's: Wage £375 per month. "Savings" £52 per month = 13.9%
>
>Mid 80's: Wage £765 per month, "Savings" £105 per month = 13.7%
>
>Mid 90's: Wage £1,725 per month, "Savings" £245 per month = 14.2%
>
>Millennium: Wage £2,860 per month, "Savings" £390 per month =13.6%
>
>2010: Wage £5,180 per month*, "Savings" £725 per month =14%
>
>*I was on an increased wage in 2010-2012 following the sale of the business
>
>Today: Wage £3,225 per month**. "Savings" £750 per month = 23%
>
>** We are currently winding down ready for retirement level spending!

Confused or what? If so, I apologise, who said money management was easy!

I think this leads nicely onto one of the next facts, because of the impact of inflation, which can be a bad thing if money is debt or isn't working for you and growing or a great thing if its compounded as income, it's very hard to get a handle on the **value of money** as its **forever changing**.

Fact 8. *The value of money is forever changing, and its either for you or against you.*

I'll use some personal anecdotes as examples that may resonate in your own homes too when talking to elders or you yourself have to relate to younger audiences in future and I'll talk a bit about how it makes a huge difference in loans and mortgages.

In my own case my mother is oft heard quoting that today's wages are ridiculously high and she managed on just **£5 a week**, or that years later my dad earned more than the Prime Minister of the UK.

I've provided some handy ready reckoners for you below so you too can check the impacts of cumulative interest, adversely or positively, on numbers yourself. I've had to go back a bit further than these tables but it would appear that my mums £5 a week equates to **£21,000 per annum** today, after allowing for inflation. Depending on whether she had that £5 after tax etc or not reveals whether it was a huge amount in its day as it's about 80% of today's average salary – I suspect it was taxed income and she was doing better than the average.

And what about my dad and the PM?

Turns out he was indeed very unusual but not alone as apparently SuperHod, aka plasterer Max *SuperHod* Quarterman hit the headlines in the 1970s when a local newspaper worked out that the hard-working plasterer earned more than Harold Wilson, the Prime Minister of the day. By the 1980s, SuperHod, below, said he was a millionaire.

SuperHod with his Rolls whereas my dad preferred Jaguars.
Picture credit The Sun/Rex Pictures.

In today's money the PM earns about six times more than the average worker, so my dad was doing **very well** indeed, and if we look at the impact of inflation (as I don't know when exactly he was on a par with SuperHod) then it would appear that my dad earned **triple my own starting wage** (I always suspected my pocket money wasn't enough!). Scaled up to today, he would still be doing about a third better than us as a family! Nice one dad.

On the plus side for us, I think we've spent a lot less and managed what we had a bit better, for example, we've relied less on "experts" for financial advice and I roughly estimate we've ended up **twice as well off** in future retirement, notwithstanding the current low interest rates which are now around 85% lower than the historic averages, so not great for investing, not as cash anyway.

So overall I guess it goes to confirm you can't have it every way, you either spend it or save it, you can't do both. But interestingly **if you save a bit you might just get the chance to spend a bit, spend again, and again, if you live long enough that is!**

In a minute I will share why all this interest rate / value of money stuff is important when looking at borrowing and saving, but before I do, here is something important that might just make it sink in a bit more.

Chapter 5

Einstein and the Power of Compounding

When researching for this book I came across the fact that Albert Einstein allegedly said that Compounded Returns, in other words cumulative interest, was the *Eighth Wonder of the World*. And who can argue with him?

So that's:

FACT 9.

And this is why Compounding Returns are important. Robert Krulwich and David Blatner explain the chessboard theory far better than I can – check out https://www.npr.orgin the appendices where the theory goes if you sold a King or an Emperor a beautiful board and instead of cash settled instead for a deal giving you one grain of wheat or rice on square one doubling to two on the next and so on, then it wouldn't be such a great deal for you would it? The King could easily afford it and in fact surely he'd have swindled you with a cheap price of just a few grains in total for a lovely chessboard?

Actually, you'd be the winner. This is because of the power of cumulative mathematics (in this case doubling up is sort of an interest rate of 100%), and by the time you reach square 64 on the board, the King would **owe more grains of rice than exist** in his kingdom, or in fact on the whole planet!

Image credit with thanks Michigan Feature

As I'm sure you can appreciate this kind of compounding or accumulating impact is fantastic if you are a **saver** with growth working for you. It's absolutely horrific if you are a borrower when it compounds against you, even more so if you don't make adequate repayments. Just look above at the pile of grains on just those squares surrounding the start point and how quickly the pile grows even when you look just a few squares into the board. And here is the mathematical proof that so impressed Einstein;

> Square 1 = 1 grain of rice or wheat
>
> Square 2 = 2 grains, Square 3 = 4 grains
>
> Square 8, end of row one = 128 grains
>
> Square 16, end of row two = 32,768 grains
>
> Square 24, end of row three = 8,388,608 grains
>
> Square 32, just **halfway** down the chessboard = 2,147,483,648 so that's **2.1 billion** grains already and we're hardly yet started.

And jumping to the end of the chessboard...

> On Square 64 we've reached **9,223,372,036,854,780,000** grains or roughly **1.1 billion grains for every single human on the planet,** and all this simply by doubling up! That would keep us going in bread or ready meals for quite some time.

FACT 10. *Never double up, on anything, especially not in a casino!*

On a related note a work colleague (who wants to remain nameless!) heard me talking about this kind of thing and decided it would be a great idea to help her saving discipline if she got herself 64 little boxes (one for each square on the chess board) and started to double up, **starting with only £0.01** and doubling every day. She thought she'd have a tidy sum in just two months' time for

Christmas presents but quickly gave up when she realised she would run out of cash. In fact she would need **100 times the total wealth of the whole planet** to complete the exercise (and the equivalent of the world's wealth would have been reached before even starting on the final row of the board!). A much more practical solution with the percentage of compounding gradually declining is simply to add a single penny every day so starting with one pence, two pence on day 2, three on day 3 and so on. This way, in two months you could still save a more affordable **£20.80**. I find it astonishing that such a small change in the arithmetic formula creates such a big change in outcome.

It's also vital here to consider that doubling up is really equating to an interest rate of 100% - In this case per square, which might in turn relate to per day in my colleague's case or per year if she had set herself the saving task over 64 years to accumulate 100 times the world's money!

> **Editor's note** – maybe that's what Jeff Bezos is up to at Amazon after all!

Somewhat surprisingly in real life here today there are **many examples of interest rates far worse than doubling up** and all that stops them getting noticed and seriously lambasted is that generally the doubling up can't continue for a very long period, simply because people do indeed run out of cash or legs to break (for example with back-street lenders and loan sharks) in the same way my colleague would have quickly run out of cash to save!

I will share a few more mainstream examples in a minute with some charts.

As a quick example, you can see on UK **TV every day of the week** adverts from lenders and loan companies quoting rates as high as **1,350% per annum**. This is an APR% so not exactly the same as a fixed interest rate (I will also say more on that) but let's just say whilst we are sort of comparing apples and pears, it is still worth noting it's a figure **way above the feared 100%.** And any rate north of 100% can't possibly be good news as it's either a high loan rate or an investment scam!

To put this 1350% or even 100% in some context, savers like pensioners today, sadly, are currently getting paid something like **0.25%** on their money, if they are lucky, so that's just **20** pence per month on each £1,000 savings, so not enough to live on. By comparison, a loan company might be making as much as **£500** a month, so **2,500 times more money on the same amount lent out to an unsuspecting borrower**. Little wonder then that they can afford to write off a few bad debts along the way and pay for expensive TV advertising.

FACT 11. – *100% in not a good thing unless its 100% Off, that is FREE*

> NB. I will come back to the topic of loan interest rates in a bit to try and explain it in greater detail and clear up some of this anomaly between apples and pears, for example, is the chessboard 100% the same as 100% APR? As a layman I don't think it is, but why not?

I promised you some handy reference tables, hopefully that might help make the point more clearly than I can explain it!

Chapter 6

Reference Tables

OK, let's use the power of cumulative interest to show the impact on money over a period of years, I'm going to choose **35 years** as most people reading this book should have 35 years left in them before it's too late to change your ways about money, if you need to change your ways in the first place that is. So if you are aged 30 now then whilst 35 years won't have taken you quite up to retirement age, any changes in money management you embark upon now could have a very big impact by then. And if you are close to retirement age already, 35 years might just be how long your money has to last you, so developing some new habits could still help!

Interest rates of course change all the time, it used to be common for the UK Base Rate or Bank Rate to change every **month** (that's kind of a benchmark rate the government, or now the Governor of the Bank of England, set and from this rate many borrowing rates are calculated).

So as an example my business might be able to borrow money at 3% over Base Rate, so if Base Rate is 0.75% as it is at the time of writing, we'd borrow at 3.75% and when Base Rate changes, so too might our cost of borrowing.

> **Editor's note** – Yes, did you know this is why people panic about their mortgage costs increasing when the Governor threatens to increase his rate, hence why people often pay a little more to fix their rate for a known period of time in advance?

Author's note — Exactly, thanks for chipping in! I like Fixed Rates and many years ago when working in the Bank said, "If Fixed Rates ever come to the UK market, I'm going Large (borrowing a lot for a big house)" and we did.

My idea was that the strength of them is that even if Base Rate drops, you know you can sleep soundly as if you can afford your mortgage when you first buy a property, you can probably also afford it tomorrow as inflation may push up your wages anyway. It's a less sound strategy these days with nobody getting pay increases in the recession.

The interest rate over the last 45 years has averaged **6.7% pa**, and in the 30 years preceding the last big recession (as that may have skewed things) it was 8.3% pa, so a lot higher than the almost **historic lows we are seeing now** at around 0.75% or less.

FACT 12.– *Your hunch could be just as good as the experts.*

In my time at the Bank I researched interest rate forecasting and discovered, to my **equal surprise and horror**, that nobody (in the Bank or any government department I could find) seemed to have a real handle as to what future interest rates would be many years ahead.

I found this odd as surely if you forward predict rates and others do the same, that consensus should go some way to leading the market rather than allowing ourselves to be blown by the winds of fate?

I discovered that whilst they planned for short periods of one, two, maybe five years, there wasn't much at the time for periods like ten, twenty, thirty years. Now I'm sure computer algorithms and futurologists have improved things in recent years but in essence it seems to be a bit of a **guessing game and your own guess may be just as good as the experts.**

In short, forward planning is a risk, so take care, but remember it is still valid to form your own opinion or hunch, just don't bet everything.

Why does this matter?

I am telling you all this before we get to the reference tables so you can understand why and how I have selected certain rates of interest

I would rather you grasp the pitfalls of my arguments and calculations than simply pick a rate from thin air and present it to you as if it were an infallible fact, as that could be dangerous.

Financial advisors do of course seemingly pluck *approved* rates from thin air when projecting how their future investments might grow, say, 7% or 12% per year being used as the basis of calculations – and they normally give you a couple of choices, but I've never yet seen one showing minus growth!

> NB. My pensions averaged 5.4% pa vs Base Rate 4.8% over the same period so they weren't what I would term a great success despite being professionally managed but I'm sure the advisors managed to extract plenty of fees along the way before I received my cut.

Even with all their skills they made me an extra 0.6% pa, that's probably a lot less than I'd have made sticking the cash in a Bank high interest account!

> NB. Past rates cannot be relied on as an example of the future, blah blah or whatever they say!

I personally would be surprised if the Base Rate in the next 30 years averages more than 2.5%, but who knows?

That's little more than a guesstimate based on past experiences.

For the purposes of the tables that follow then let's **use instead the last 35 years of real rates** to make our calculations more realistic in terms of demonstrating **fluctuation** through a period of years, as it shows it can be surprisingly volatile.

And going forward, as past examples cannot be relied on when planning the future (as history may not repeat itself!), I will simply use a slowly growing steady rate starting from today.

The data in this first Reference Table then leads us nicely onto:

FACT 13. *Table 1. It's Dangerous Doing Nothing or Paying Interest.*

TABLE 1

	Interest Rate	Spending Power/No Pay Increase	Normal Savings Account	High Interest Account	Bank Borrowing BR + 5% (authorised)	Borrowed at 3% pm Credit Union	Borrowed @ 150% Pay Day Loan - No charges
	BR	Inflation = -BR	BR + 0.3%	BR + 4%			
		£	£	£	£	£	£
Year 1	10.0%	10,000	10,000	10,000	10,000	10,000	10,000
		£	£	£	£	£	£
Year 2	12.5%	9,000	11,280	11,650	11,750	13,600	25,000
		£	£	£	£	£	£
Year 3	11.0%	7,875	12,555	13,398	13,630	18,496	62,500
		£	£	£	£	£	£
Year 4	9.4%	7,009	13,772	15,193	15,593	25,155	156,250
		£	£	£	£	£	
Year 5	9.5%	6,350	15,122	17,244	17,854	34,210	
		£	£	£	£	£	
Year 6	14.0%	5,747	17,285	20,348	21,246	46,526	
		£	£	£	£	£	
Year 7	13.9%	4,942	19,739	23,990	25,261	63,275	
		£	£	£	£		
Year 8	11.9%	4,255	22,147	27,804	29,530	86,054	
		£	£	£	£	£	
Year 9	8.4%	3,749	24,074	31,252	33,488	117,034	
		£	£	£	£	£	
Year 10	5.6%	3,434	25,494	34,252	37,037	159,166	
		£	£	£	£	£	
Year 11	5.6%	3,242	26,999	37,540	40,963	216,466	
		£	£	£	£		
Year 12	6.5%	3,060	28,834	41,482	45,674		
		£	£	£	£	NB. Max rate allowed	NB. Loans can't run this long
Year 13	5.9%	2,861	30,622	45,589	50,652	Not all credit unions can	but borrowers do tend to
		£	£	£	£		reborrow
Year 14	6.8%	2,692	32,796	50,513	56,629	lend for ten years.	frequently
		£	£	£	£		
Year 15	6.9%	2,509	35,158	56,018	63,368		
		£	£	£	£		
Year 16	5.4%	2,336	37,162	61,284	69,959		
		£	£	£	£		
Year 17	5.9%	2,210	39,466	67,351	77,584		
		£	£	£	£		
Year 18	5.5%	2,080	41,755	73,750	85,730		
		£	£	£	£		
Year 19	5.0%	1,965	43,968	80,387	94,304		
		£	£	£	£		
Year 20	4.0%	1,867	45,858	86,818	102,791		
		£	£	£	£		
Year 21	3.7%	1,792	47,693	93,503	111,734		
		£	£	£	£		
Year 22	4.4%	1,726	49,934	101,357	122,237		
		£	£	£	£		
Year 23	4.5%	1,650	52,331	109,573	133,849		
		£	£	£	£		
Year 24	4.9%	1,576	55,052	119,760	147,100		
		£	£	£	£		
Year 25	4.0%	1,489	57,419	129,341	160,389		
		£	£	£	£		
Year 26	1.0%	1,439	58,166	135,808	169,959		
		£	£	£	£		
Year 27	0.5%	1,424	58,631	141,919	179,307		
		£	£	£	£		
Year 28	0.5%	1,417	59,100	148,306	188,169		
		£	£	£	£		
Year 29	0.5%	1,410	59,573	154,980	199,573		
		£	£	£	£		
Year 30	0.5%	1,403	60,050	161,954	210,550		
		£	£	£	£		
Year 31	0.5%	1,396	60,530	169,242	222,130		
		£	£	£	£		
Year 32	0.5%	1,389	61,014	176,857	234,347		
		£	£	£	£		
Year 33	0.3%	1,382	61,380	184,462	246,768		
		£	£	£	£		
Year 34	0.5%	1,378	61,871	192,763	260,340		
		£	£	£	£		
Year 35	0.6%	1,371	62,444	201,678	274,984		

In column 3 in Table 1 I have calculated how a salary gets eroded each year by inflation (its spending power decreases even though the amount of money is unchanged) so this shows the estimated **value** in future but using today's amount of money, as products and services will be more expensive by then.

So, say, a £10,000 pa salary erodes to being worth the equivalent of just £9,000 in one year if the inflation that year is 10% so you lose out quickly if you forget to ask for pay increases or put your money under the mattress and its equivalent value is just **£1,371** in 35 years' time (Remember we are re-using the rates of history to project forwards as nobody can predict the future.)

Whereas in column 4 I have calculated how that same £10,000 would grow in absolute terms if it were saved, firstly in a fairly standard savings account paying around 0.3% above Base Rate pa at a Bank or Building Society. Column 5 shows the significant improvement that could be achieved instead in a higher rate account at, say, zopa.com where you might earn around 4.5% pre-tax today.

> NB. So over the same 35 years the £10,000 could grow to either £62,000 or £202,000 depending on where it's invested. Whether that will purchase the same as £10,000 today depends on whether products and services keep up with the real rate of inflation or not. Again, it's a guesstimate, but what's certain is if you invest your money you will have a better chance of affording the same things in the future as you can afford now, and if you do well in your investing, as we have done, you can buy more (or give it away to good causes, whatever you choose).

FACT 14. – *Inflation will erode your spending power unless you save and invest.*

In the right hand columns 6-8 I have for comparison shown some examples regarding what happens on the opposite side of the coin, if you are a borrower and for the purposes of easier comparison I have assumed repayments are **not** being made. So in column 6 look how a debt grows even at a low rate typically charged by a UK **Bank** to someone with a decent credit rating, so at today's rates that's around 5.5% EAR/AER which stands for an effective annual rate (as they often charge interest daily and you need to understand the annual impact).

In column 7 we have the maximum rate and period allowed to be offered by a **Credit Union**, a useful source of cheapish borrowing for people with less good credit ratings, and some credit unions will lend up to ten years.

And in the final column a pretty typical rate for a **Pay Day** lender although note that they won't usually lend £10,000 nor allow it to roll on without repayments for 3 years as a) nobody could afford it due to the power of cumulative mathematics and b) thank goodness it's being legislated against in the UK.

But of course people cheat and re-borrow so whilst these lenders may officially be limited to £2,000 lent over 14 months plus a maximum 0.8% interest **per day**, who knows for sure how closely that's adhered to? Anyway that's still a huge rate of interest (per day, not per month or year) and for the purposes of these examples I haven't even added in the extra charges they can legally add on alongside the interest.

So the message that this is **hugely expensive** is I think generally fair.

To hopefully bring this comparison to life as they don't all extend for 35 years, for ease I have highlighted in grey a **threshold number that reappears in each scenario**, but at very different points in time - so remember **£60,000 and that we started with just £10,000**

So in the first savings columns you can see that over **35 years**, even at a very low interest rates **£10,000 can grow to over £62,000** whereas if an imaginary saver had taken just a few moments of extra hassle to seek out a slightly better rate in a higher paying account, the £62k would have been reached in around **half the time**, at just 16 years....**that leads us to:**

FACT 15. – *Just a few minutes of research will save you 19 years or thousands of pounds.*

With borrowing the change in impact on finances is even more dramatic.

A £10,000 **debt reaches £63,000 in just 14 years**, and that's at a very **low, that is** cheap, interest rate from a Bank. It escalates even quicker in just **half** that time at a supposedly *cheap* credit union.

Most amazing of all, if it were possible, a £10,000 debt could reach nearly £63,000 in a staggering **two years** with a Pay Day lender.

A more realistic smaller loan, say of £1,000 could still become £6,300 if borrowed at a Pay Day Lender for just two years.

The message to me seems to be a clear one. Ensure you:

- Always ask for your pay increases!
- Save what you can when you can.
- Try never to use credit or loans unless it's for important asset, and preferably one that will increase in value not decline as furniture or a normal car does. I touch on

this topic in more detail in the mortgage section and when I think is the right and wrong time to buy a house.
- And as I said in the introduction, if you can it makes sense to use someone else's money – if at all possible let them pay the interest and take the risk (for things like a business) if at all possible (provided it doesn't put too much risk on your own assets through things like guarantees or mortgages – but that's a book in itself!).

Here's another handy reference table to enable you to talk to elderly relatives or your own young children about the importance of saving!

In Table 2 you can work backwards looking at the impact of inflation on the value of £10 35 years ago (now worth £1.36) or £10 now (was worth £73.40) or Table 3 shows how it grows if invested.

Tables 2 and 3

Base Rate or Future Estimate	YEARS BACK	TABLE 2 THEN	NOW	FUTURE	TABLE 3 THEN	NOW	FUTURE
							Inflation Impact / Investment Impact (BR +4%)
11.0%	-35	£ 10.00	£ 73.40	£ 184.52	£ 10.00	£ 0.40	£ 0.04
10.0%	-34	£ 9.00	£ 66.06	£ 166.07	£ 11.50	£ 0.46	£ 0.05
12.5%	-33	£ 7.87	£ 57.80	£ 145.31	£ 13.11	£ 0.52	£ 0.06
11.0%	-32	£ 7.01	£ 51.44	£ 129.33	£ 15.27	£ 0.60	£ 0.07
9.4%	-31	£ 6.35	£ 46.61	£ 117.17	£ 17.56	£ 0.70	£ 0.08
9.5%	-30	£ 5.75	£ 42.18	£ 106.04	£ 19.92	£ 0.79	£ 0.09
14.0%	-29	£ 4.94	£ 36.27	£ 91.19	£ 22.61	£ 0.89	£ 0.10
13.9%	-28	£ 4.26	£ 31.23	£ 78.52	£ 26.68	£ 1.06	£ 0.12
11.9%	-27	£ 3.75	£ 27.52	£ 69.17	£ 31.45	£ 1.25	£ 0.14
8.4%	-26	£ 3.43	£ 25.20	£ 63.36	£ 36.45	£ 1.44	£ 0.16
5.6%	-25	£ 3.24	£ 23.79	£ 59.82	£ 40.97	£ 1.62	£ 0.18
5.6%	-24	£ 3.06	£ 22.46	£ 56.47	£ 44.90	£ 1.78	£ 0.20
6.5%	-23	£ 2.86	£ 21.00	£ 52.80	£ 49.22	£ 1.95	£ 0.22
5.9%	-22	£ 2.69	£ 19.76	£ 49.68	£ 54.38	£ 2.15	£ 0.24
6.8%	-21	£ 2.51	£ 18.42	£ 46.30	£ 59.77	£ 2.37	£ 0.26
6.9%	-20	£ 2.34	£ 17.15	£ 43.11	£ 66.22	£ 2.62	£ 0.29
5.4%	-19	£ 2.21	£ 16.22	£ 40.78	£ 73.44	£ 2.91	£ 0.32
5.9%	-18	£ 2.08	£ 15.26	£ 38.37	£ 80.34	£ 3.18	£ 0.35
5.5%	-17	£ 1.97	£ 14.42	£ 36.26	£ 88.30	£ 3.50	£ 0.39
5.0%	-16	£ 1.87	£ 13.70	£ 34.45	£ 96.69	£ 3.83	£ 0.42
4.0%	-15	£ 1.79	£ 13.16	£ 33.07	£ 105.39	£ 4.17	£ 0.46
3.7%	-14	£ 1.73	£ 12.67	£ 31.85	£ 113.82	£ 4.51	£ 0.50
4.4%	-13	£ 1.65	£ 12.11	£ 30.45	£ 122.58	£ 4.85	£ 0.54
4.5%	-12	£ 1.58	£ 11.57	£ 29.08	£ 132.88	£ 5.26	£ 0.58
4.9%	-11	£ 1.50	£ 11.00	£ 27.65	£ 144.17	£ 5.71	£ 0.63
4.0%	-10	£ 1.44	£ 10.56	£ 26.55	£ 157.01	£ 6.22	£ 0.69
1.0%	-9	£ 1.42	£ 10.45	£ 26.28	£ 169.57	£ 6.71	£ 0.74
0.5%	-8	£ 1.42	£ 10.40	£ 26.15	£ 178.04	£ 7.05	£ 0.78
0.5%	-7	£ 1.41	£ 10.35	£ 26.02	£ 186.06	£ 7.37	£ 0.82
0.5%	-6	£ 1.40	£ 10.30	£ 25.89	£ 194.43	£ 7.70	£ 0.85
0.5%	-5	£ 1.40	£ 10.25	£ 25.76	£ 203.18	£ 8.04	£ 0.89
0.5%	-4	£ 1.39	£ 10.19	£ 25.63	£ 212.32	£ 8.41	£ 0.93
0.5%	-3	£ 1.38	£ 10.14	£ 25.50	£ 221.88	£ 8.78	£ 0.97
0.3%	-2	£ 1.38	£ 10.11	£ 25.43	£ 231.86	£ 9.18	£ 1.02
0.5%	-1	£ 1.37	£ 10.06	£ 25.30	£ 241.83	£ 9.57	£ 1.06
0.6%	NOW	£ 1.36	£ 10.00	£ 25.14	£ 252.71	£ 10.00	£ 1.11

In Table 4 below we are looking into the future (so the interest rates are my estimates which are much lower than the past reality) and again you can see how in another 35 years that original £10.00 now worth £1.36 may shrink further to just 54 pence in equivalent spending power and how £10 now could shrink to just £3.98 or grow to £90.22 if invested instead. So as you can see, savers will prosper in comparison.

Table 4 and Table 5

Base Rate or Future Estimate	YEARS FUTURE	TABLE 4 Inflation Impact			TABLE 5 Investment Impact (BR +4%)		
		PAST	NOW	FUTURE	PAST	NOW	FUTURE
1.0%	NOW	£ 1.36	£ 10.00	£ 25.14	£ 252.71	£ 10.00	£ 1.11
0.8%	+1	£ 1.35	£ 9.92	£ 24.93	£ 264.40	£ 10.47	£ 1.16
1.0%	+2	£ 1.34	£ 9.82	£ 24.70	£ 277.16	£ 10.97	£ 1.22
1.1%	+3	£ 1.32	£ 9.72	£ 24.43	£ 290.88	£ 11.52	£ 1.28
1.2%	+4	£ 1.31	£ 9.60	£ 24.14	£ 305.64	£ 12.10	£ 1.34
1.3%	+5	£ 1.29	£ 9.48	£ 23.83	£ 321.53	£ 12.73	£ 1.41
1.4%	+6	£ 1.27	£ 9.35	£ 23.50	£ 338.49	£ 13.40	£ 1.49
1.5%	+7	£ 1.25	£ 9.21	£ 23.14	£ 356.77	£ 14.12	£ 1.57
1.6%	+8	£ 1.23	£ 9.06	£ 22.77	£ 376.39	£ 14.90	£ 1.65
1.7%	+9	£ 1.21	£ 8.90	£ 22.38	£ 397.47	£ 15.74	£ 1.74
1.8%	+10	£ 1.19	£ 8.74	£ 21.98	£ 420.13	£ 16.63	£ 1.84
1.9%	+11	£ 1.17	£ 8.58	£ 21.57	£ 444.50	£ 17.60	£ 1.95
2.0%	+12	£ 1.15	£ 8.41	£ 21.13	£ 470.72	£ 18.64	£ 2.07
2.1%	+13	£ 1.12	£ 8.23	£ 20.69	£ 498.96	£ 19.75	£ 2.19
2.2%	+14	£ 1.10	£ 8.05	£ 20.24	£ 529.40	£ 20.96	£ 2.32
2.3%	+15	£ 1.07	£ 7.86	£ 19.77	£ 562.22	£ 22.26	£ 2.47
2.4%	+16	£ 1.05	£ 7.68	£ 19.30	£ 597.64	£ 23.66	£ 2.62
2.5%	+17	£ 1.02	£ 7.48	£ 18.81	£ 635.89	£ 25.18	£ 2.79
2.6%	+18	£ 0.99	£ 7.29	£ 18.32	£ 677.23	£ 26.81	£ 2.97
2.7%	+19	£ 0.97	£ 7.09	£ 17.83	£ 721.92	£ 28.58	£ 3.17
2.8%	+20	£ 0.94	£ 6.89	£ 17.32	£ 770.29	£ 30.50	£ 3.38
2.9%	+21	£ 0.91	£ 6.69	£ 16.83	£ 822.67	£ 32.57	£ 3.61
3.0%	+22	£ 0.88	£ 6.49	£ 16.32	£ 879.44	£ 34.82	£ 3.86
3.1%	+23	£ 0.86	£ 6.29	£ 15.82	£ 941.00	£ 37.25	£ 4.13
3.2%	+24	£ 0.83	£ 6.09	£ 15.31	£ 1,007.81	£ 39.90	£ 4.42
3.3%	+25	£ 0.80	£ 5.89	£ 14.80	£ 1,080.37	£ 42.77	£ 4.74
3.4%	+26	£ 0.78	£ 5.69	£ 14.30	£ 1,159.24	£ 45.88	£ 5.09
3.5%	+27	£ 0.75	£ 5.49	£ 13.80	£ 1,245.02	£ 49.29	£ 5.46
3.6%	+28	£ 0.72	£ 5.29	£ 13.30	£ 1,338.40	£ 52.99	£ 5.87
3.7%	+29	£ 0.69	£ 5.10	£ 12.81	£ 1,440.11	£ 57.01	£ 6.32
3.8%	+30	£ 0.67	£ 4.90	£ 12.33	£ 1,551.00	£ 61.40	£ 6.81
3.9%	+31	£ 0.64	£ 4.71	£ 11.84	£ 1,671.98	£ 66.19	£ 7.34
4.0%	+32	£ 0.62	£ 4.52	£ 11.37	£ 1,804.07	£ 71.42	£ 7.92
4.1%	+33	£ 0.59	£ 4.34	£ 10.90	£ 1,948.39	£ 77.14	£ 8.55
4.2%	+34	£ 0.57	£ 4.16	£ 10.45	£ 2,106.21	£ 83.38	£ 9.24
4.3%	+35	£ 0.54	£ 3.98	£ 10.00	£ 2,278.92	£ 90.22	£ 10.00

So just to check that makes sense, £10 invested 35 years ago and maintained in a decent higher earning account (so it would have needed to be moved around fairly regularly as the Banks and savings institutions drop rates regularly to catch us out) would have been worth circa £252.71 today and maybe £2,278.92 in another 35 years. Not bad for £10, no wonder the Royal Family are so wealthy after all these years!

> **Editor's note** – It's funny you should say that (about Banks not the Royal Family). I've noticed how I might take out the Super-Dooper-High-Interest Account paying 4% today and before I know it the Bank has dropped the rate well below base rate to something like a derisory 0.01% pa. So £10,000 would now earn me £1 per year before tax instead of £400, yippee!

> **Author's note** – Absolutely, it's one of the most popular tricks. They do of course tell us about the rate reduction, and it's not just the Banks, but what annoys me is they know few of us will take notice and less still will take action. In fact they rely on that. I don't mind that, it's business. But what really annoys me is they still call it the Sooper-Dooper-High-Interest Account and haven't got the ethics or decency to change the name to something nearer to what-it-does-in-the-tin** such as the Really-Cr*p-Super-Low-Interest Account. We wouldn't miss taking action then! Interestingly I did once write to a Bank Director about this, but obviously they declined to comment or act!

> **Editor again** - ****We'd better acknowledge Ronseal for that!**

One way of using these tables is for price comparisons. For example let's say your parents purchased an XR2 Ford Fiesta in 1984 for £5,733, its new price then, or thereabouts. That's 34 years ago so in column 1 in Table 2, £10 was worth £9.00 by then and at the foot of that column you can see its only worth £1.36 now. So to calculate how much that XR2 should be today, divide £1.36 into £9.00 (= £6.62) and multiply that by the cost then, £5,733, to arrive at today's inflation adjusted price of £37,938. A comparable car today might be the Fiesta Mk8 ST Line which actually costs a mere £17,165, so amazingly **less than half the adjusted value** of the XR2, a car which would obviously have a lower specification and technology than the latest models 34 years later. It just goes to show how efficient modern manufacturing is and hence maybe why so many people think they can afford nice cars.

> **Editor's note** – Or is it efficient really? Have you heard how you can have a bit of fun comparing prices to confectionery, as other than occasional size changes, it is a remarkably stable predictor of real value and affordability as the industry is always innovating to reduce costs and to compete. So it's a good bell-weather generally. In your above XR2 example if we divide the original car cost of £5,733 by the approximate price of a Mars Bar then in 1984 (£0.37p I recall) you'll see you could theoretically buy that car for circa 15,500 chocolate bars instead of cash. Jump forward to today (not that you could if you'd eaten all that chocolate) and after allowing for weight changes (as bars have shrunk), a same size Mars Bar today would on average cost £0.48p (confectionary and food is much cheaper proportionately than it was) so instead of spending the £17,165 value you

calculated today a comparable new car could be acquired for 35,760 chocolate bars. So maybe in real terms cars are a lot more expensive, more than double in fact!

And even if you paid the top price for your chocolate (you could pay 90p for a small Mars Bar now but who would?) then you'd still need 19,000 bars, so even using the best figures makes the newer car 20% more expensive (in chocolate trading terms) than back in 1984. **So is it such good value after all?**

> **Author's note** – maybe that explains all the extra gizmos on cars today? They could be made a lot cheaper due to advances in manufacturing and technology (as Dacia and MG are doing) but the manufacturers keep on adding more features to keep the prices up?

PS. All this talk of inflation and increased car costs has depressed me and left me in need of a few Mars Bars, whatever the cost!

OK, I've probably said enough about Interest rates, you get it! You can work for you or against you at a surprising rate and all thanks to our pal Mr Einstein's favourite theorem (other than his own).

Before we move on let me just say that the importance of this section was simply to reinforce how **seemingly small changes in rates, whether you are earning interest, or paying it, add up to huge lifestyle implications** down the line. It really is worth taking a few minutes to research costs and rates. I will have more to say on the subject for sure but don't worry, it could save you **£100,000** so don't quit on me just yet!

Chapter 7

Lots of Accounts

To put all this this monkeying around with different interest rates into some context for you, in researching this book I have looked through our financial records of many live and lapsed accounts. But have a guess how many different accounts we've had over 40 years? A handful, a dozen, two dozen? (Account in this context also means an individual investment but I'm not counting each share I've held as one, the account itself numbers one but if we owned twenty shares within it, it's still one for the purposes of this calculation!).

The answer may surprise you, it surprised me:

135 accounts / investments!

That's how many we have had over 40 or so years, and I bet I've missed a few along the way too, albeit not the most significant ones. So the reality is probably that we've had nearer 160 accounts, savings or investments.

That means I'm opening a new, let's call it an Account, **every 3 months or so**. I'm often also closing one down too of course and shifting the money about as it's all about **moving money and debt around into the most favourable rates**. You have to keep on the ball or the financial intuitions will steal your lunch money, literally. This leads on to:

FACT 16. – *I would worry if I'd held an account without checking its performance at least once per year (unless it's a Fixed Rate deal like a 2 Year 2.4% ISA)*

Chapter 8

What about mortgages? I said they are significant?

Mortgages are nothing special other than for most people your home represents your largest single transaction but they are also worthy of special mention as of course these are the type of account we tend to take out for the **longest period** of time. It's therefore worth considering them specifically as people are generally happy to trust the l**ocal broker or office** to do us a good deal and or leave things ticking along for year after year without much shopping around, either pre-purchase or during the mortgage term itself. This **isn't a healthy situation**.

With mortgages, my understanding is that interest can be calculated in various subtly different ways, typically on the balance outstanding at the end of the day, which may therefore reduce as you gradually repay a small amount of the loan each month (unless it's an interest only loan when you clear the whole debt on the last day, assuming you can find the money from somewhere, such as an investment bond). Whereas with a typical personal loan, for example used for home improvements or a car purchase, the total interest is calculated on Day 1 and you pay a small increment of interest off each month. It can make a difference, especially if you pay chunks off early.

Whilst mortgage rates seem like a cheap source of borrowing as for most people the rates are a lot lower than say a Bank overdraft rate (so it's tempting to borrow more than you need on a mortgage or re-mortgage , often **adding on a small extra bit** for a car or holiday). But because the period of the loan is so lengthy, a huge amount of interest will be paid in total making even that small addition into a large amount.

Fact 17. — *The Total Amount to be Repaid is therefore one of the most important things to check. I think it's the most important as it also includes all the charges.*

> **Editor's note** – in my day you couldn't do this, you could only borrow towards the house cost, not even furnishings or legal costs could be added on.
>
> **Author's note** — That's right, it's more generous in some ways now. When I worked in Banking in the 80's we even had to ask to see proof of how the funds were spent with receipts for example. And you could also only take out so much cash out of the country for your holiday!

In our own case, whilst house prices today are at least **10 X more expensive** than when we started out on the property ladder, a typical mortgage rate today is not far off **90% cheaper** (we were paying around 16%, and Base Rate was 15%, whereas today Base Rate is 0.75% and it's not unusual to see mortgages below 2.5%). So proportionally it is all probably pretty similar – wages are higher now due to the aforementioned cumulative interest graphs!

Overall no one generation is probably that much better off than another when it comes to acquiring property (the cost of living is also higher now) and, yes, today's pensioners did get cheap houses but they paid a lot for their money (and could typically only include one wage in the affordability calculations) whereas youngsters today can include more income sources and borrow at very cheap rates, but the upkeep and living costs are so much more.

Today it is possible to borrow over much longer periods (I was shocked to see 40 years when doing the research whereas in my days as a Banker it was generally capped at 25 years. I know a long period seems great but **who wants to be paying off a loan at 70? – we wanted to stop by our mid-40s to give us more life choices.**

Hopefully as you will realise in a minute, it doesn't make economic sense to pay for this long either, but it's great news for the lenders hence all those big profits!

All this adds up to reinforce to me why it's a good discipline to save and keep putting money in the right places, so **not under the mattress.**

Choosing your mortgage wisely is important as even small changes in the fees, APRs (Annual Percentage Rate) or timescales before the rate can change (fixed period) or the overall loan length, will have a huge impact on the total amount you have to pay back.

In the example that follows (Table 6) I have picked an imaginary example mortgage of just **£100,000** to buy a property worth £170,000 using a Capital Repayment mortgage that each month pays off the interest owed and a small amount of the capital borrowed, hence the name, whereas a cheaper Interest Only loan only pays back the interest, leaving the borrower to settle the Capital later. With a **Capital Repayment** Mortgage by the time the borrower is in, say, the last year of the mortgage, almost nothing, (maybe 1%) of the original debt remains, whereas in a cheaper interest only deal 100% of the original debt needs to be found. The good news is that in future that £100,000 won't seem worth much due to the adverse impact of inflation.

As you can probably guess we have personally always preferred the old fashioned Capital Repayment mortgages as you have a better handle on where you are at any point in time and if rates were to shoot up or if I'd been made redundant or taken ill suddenly then at least we would have paid a proportion of the original debt off. And even if it's only a small amount that's repaid it's better than nothing. It's nice too to feel that gradually you are increasing the percentage equity that you own in your own home instead of the lender owning it, theoretically.

OK, so back to our imaginary lender borrowing £100,000.

I have rounded up the monthly payments and total amounts repayable with three of the **currently cheapest lenders** as listed on MoneySupermarket.com on 9/7/2018. It's interesting (to me) to note that even with relatively small differences in interest rate and APR percentages between **the top providers**, the final amounts repayable can vary by a **huge amount**, and also that the **best deals aren't always at the top of the list** – so you need to shop around despite the re-assurances comparison websites may give you.

So at the time of researching, the best deals were with the Nationwide and on a 40 year deal the monthly costs differed even between the cheapest lenders by £45 a month. That's a potential saving of almost **10% each month**. Over the full term this could save a borrower **£19,500**, see Table 6 below.

I daren't check in detail **how much worse** the more expensive providers would be but a quick overview suggests that over even a short period like 13 years the interest paid would **more than double** (and the monthly payment would be **20% higher**) and on the maximum 40 year term it would cost the borrower a staggering **additional £95,000** in interest and almost **40% more each month.**

So on £100,000 of borrowing they would have to repay £100,000 plus £190,000 in interest and other charges equating to an APR% of 7% (versus 3.4% at the cheaper lenders)!

So remember to shop around thoroughly and consider using a no fee broker to help in your search (they get commission paid by the lender, not you).

Table 6

TABLE 6 Capital & Interest Repayment Type			Mortgages £100,000 Loan, £170,000 Property Valuation			
		Progressive B/Soc	Cumberland B/Soc	Nationwide		SAVINGS
40 Years						
	Monthly	£455	£440	£410		£45
	Total Paid	£ 213,500	£207,500	£194,000		£ 19,500
	APR	4.4%	4.2%	3.8%		0.6%
30 Years						
	Monthly	£505	£490	£465		£40
	Total Paid	£ 183,000	£175,000	£166,000		£ 17,000
	APR	4.2%	4.1%	3.7%		0.5%
20 Years						
	Monthly	£625	£615	£590		£35
	Total Paid	£ 146,500	£145,000	£140,000		£ 6,500
	APR	4.0%	4.0%	3.6%		0.4%
15 Years						
	Monthly	£750	£740	£720		£30
	Total Paid	£ 132,000	£131,500	£128,000		£ 4,000
	APR	3.8%	3.8%	3.5%		0.3%
13 years						
	Monthly	£830	£825	£800		£30
	Total Paid	£ 126,500	£126,000	£123,500		£ 3,000
	APR	3.7%	3.7%	3.4%		0.3%

Reducing monthly fee by:	£ 390	-49%
Increases the term by:	27 years	68%
And increases costs by:	£70,500	400%

What is more shocking to me than the disparity between the cheapest and best lenders or even between just the top lenders rates competing with each other are the numbers at the foot of the page, I discovered this when working in a Bank all those years ago and it is almost as true now as it was then. This is what I learnt.

FACT 18. – *Pretend for a minute that you could afford to double your monthly repayments. The loan isn't repaid in half of the time, the period drops by two thirds or more.*

And it's all because of that fact that Einstein admired, in this case, the adverse impact of cumulative mathematics.

Well it is almost the same today and even if in real life you can't double your repayments (let's face it, who can?) certainly **don't try and cut the monthly cost by adding to the length of the loan period, as this opposite effect will cost you dearly**.

- As an example, being tempted to cut the monthly outgoings (say from £800 down to £410) may seem like a great idea, but it will generally increase the loan period by 68% from 13 years to a depressing 40 years. And the overall cost will add up to around **400% more overall**, that's £70,500 in extra interest.

So whilst I'm not suggesting that anyone buying a house today could afford to double the repayments, as Table 6 shows even a small extra payment, say from £410 (highlighted) up to just £465 a month **could cut ten years from the loan** with the same lender, that is from 40 years down to 30 years, would **save £28,000** in overall costs (as the total repaid drops from £194,000 to £166,000. This is with the best lender in the example, the savings are even greater if we'd picked one of the more expensive lenders.

Before we move on from this section I will leave you with some background information about rate fluctuations that may be interesting:

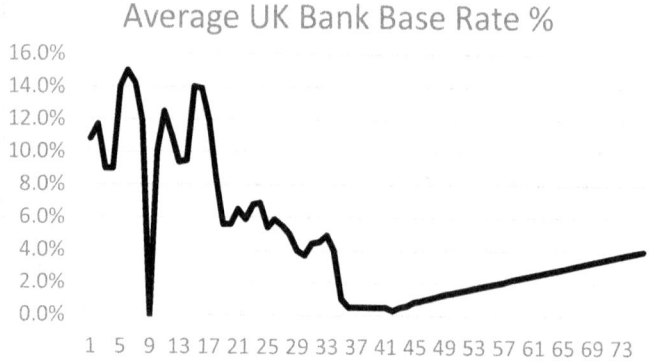

This graph shows an actual record of how the UK Bank Base Rate, which impacts other borrowing and saving rates, has **varied** a lot of the last 40 or so years, proving how hard it is for anyone to predict anything with complete safety. In the second half of the graph I have plotted just for comparison how I think it might perform in the next 35 years, although obviously it won't be such a simple straight trend line as I have shown. And what do I know anyway!

All I'm hoping to reinforce from this is that this shows that the future rates I've used in my Reference Tables are pretty modest versus past rates and so could conceivably be modest in comparison to future rates. If things fluctuate in future as they have in the past then the impact on saving or borrowing in future could be **even more dramatic** (for good and bad) than my examples earlier in the book have highlighted.

FACT? *Possibly not but to me this again suggests strongly that the time for action is now, don't delay saving or paying down debt.*

Chapter 9

In pictures too

Before we move on I realise that many people are not comfortable with words or numbers and prefer a visual way of learning – so here is a graph that attempts to bring together in one place examples of what happens to money if you don't invest it (shrinks in value) versus how it grows if you invest.

And let's not forget how it goes up even more if you borrow so you end up paying back more. Even a small loan today from a seemingly reputable company can be a big problem just a few short years down the line, even more so if you don't keep up repayments.

> **Editor's note** - I would have put the graph in colour to make it easier to read but colour printing would make the book more expensive to buy and this is all about saving money, not wasting it so you will have to just check the key re which dotted line is which carefully! From left to right the graph is

Pay-Day Loan, Bank Loan, Bank Savings Account, Under the Mattress/Do Nothing.

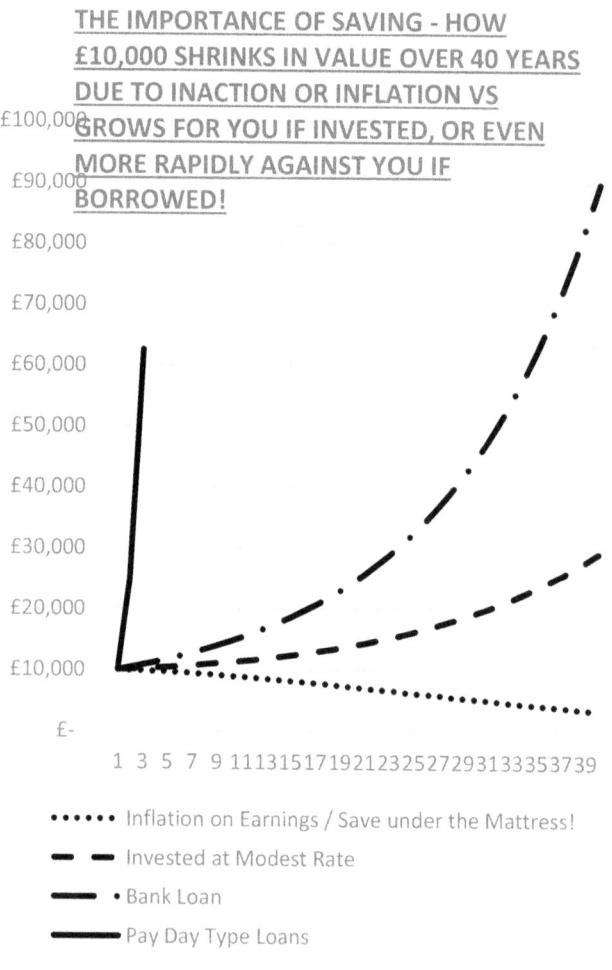

Chapter 10
APR's and Confusing Stuff

When I worked in banking their seemed to be no clear guidance regarding how these rates, intended to remove confusion for customers, were calculated, in short, the methodology could vary, hence comparisons were pretty useless. I don't think it's improved a lot and I suspect 90% of the public don't understand any of this anyway, or things like EARs, APRCs, Fixed rates and so on. To make matters worse, I think I'm correct in saying that it's not as simple as saying 1200% APR is always 12 times worse than 100% Fixed Rate – but it might possibly always be 600% or six times worse, so beware when borrowing if you see any big numbers.

What lies behind all this is a laudable intent of our politicians to stop us being hoodwinked by unscrupulous lenders and to give us a simple way to compare the **Cost of Money**. But because there are so many types of finance and so many differing legitimate charges, it makes the calculations so varied as to make comparisons almost worthless. Plus of course even good lenders will play with these variations and invent new product characteristics to make sure their product stands out favourably in a crowded market, but it doesn't really help consumers much IMHO.

I tend to think that three things are worth focusing on:

- If you are borrowing, big percentages are always bad whereas they are good if you are a saver. But in general, any really **big number is going to either be bad or a scam, so avoid it**. Big in this context could be 40%, so not even 400%.

- The **TOTAL** figures are often most useful, that is how much you need to repay in total or how much you will earn and get back, in Total. It's no different really to going to the races. You want to know if you bet £1 and win, you get your £ back plus £0.70, or if you lose, you lose just £1.
- If you like numbers, then the real % rate being applied (i.e. if you tried to do the maths yourself) **will often be around half of the APR** or other rate quoted (but not always).

So as an example if I was applying for a Bank Loan at 6% APR, irrespective of what rates they claim, I will tend to assume this may well be costing only 3% in real money.

So on say a £1,000 loan it might cost just £30 in interest plus a small £5 set up fee, which might in total not seem so bad if you have an urgent problem to solve short term.

The APR may make it look worse, say 6%, simply because of the way interest is calculated and the fact that you won't owe the full £1,000 for the full period.

Confusion abounds.

I'm just interested it costs me £35 to solve a problem.

Here are some real life examples from the markets today:

Table 7

TABLE 7

OFFICIAL DATA   AVERAGE WAGE MILLIONAIRE CALCULATIONS

	A	B	C	D	E	F	G	H	I	J	K
Lender	Amount	Repaid (Total)	Period (Mths)	Fixed Rate	APR	Interest (B-A)	Interest/ Mth (F/C)	Monthly Rate (G/A)	Rate * 12 ($H*12$)	Double ($I/0.5$)	Diff (J-D)
Sunny	£200	£382	6	292%	1291%	£182	£30.33	15.2%	182.0%	364.0%	-72%
Log Book Loans	£850	£2,533	18	132%	450%	£1,683	£93.50	11.0%	132.0%	264.0%	-132%
HSBC	£3,000	£3,874	36	19%	19%	£874	£24.28	0.8%	9.7%	19.4%	-1%
Zopa	£7,500	£9,443	60	9%	10%	£1,943	£32.38	0.4%	5.2%	10.4%	-2%

Interest per month to HSBC or Zopa is comparable to Sunny but the amount borrowed is 15-37 times more with the lower cost lenders!

I believe I am right in saying the government would like you to take notice of columns D (Fixed Rate) and in particular E (The Annual Percentage Rate) which purports to be the cost of money. So in this case HSBC are around 20%. As you can see Log Book Loans, despite being secured against a vehicle, are 22 times more expensive than the Bank. Sunny Pay Day loans are around 65 times more expensive.

But many people are indeed swayed by the Fixed Rates the lenders also quote as these sound less confusing, and these are generally a lot lower. The Bank indeed appears to be twice as expensive as Zopa (Zopa is a peer to peer lender and you can borrow or save money there), whereas Log Book loans only appear to be 6.5 times more expensive than the Bank and Sunny 14 times. But are they cheating? Who knows?

In practice I do my own calculation which attempts to level the playfield so at least I have a chance of deciding for myself. I do it like this (see Table 7):

- Firstly I deduct the total repaid from the amount borrowed, to see how much the **lender is charging** and I then divide this by the period, so all loans are then comparable.
- I then divide the answer by the loan amount to arrive at my estimate of the **monthly interest rate**, this is then multiplied to give an estimated annual rate.
- And finally I go back to my comment about APRs being double the real rate, so I double my answer to give me something to **compare** to the quoted rates.

In Column K you will see I am looking at the difference between my estimated rate in (Column J) and the lenders' own claimed Fixed Rate (Column D). As expected my calculation is pretty spot on for the Bank and Zopa, just 1-2% out, and its perhaps no coincidence that these are the most ethical lenders (Zopa is soon to be a Bank) likely to stick to the spirit of the law.

I'm not of course saying that the shorter term more expensive lenders are any less ethical but I find it interesting to note that this is where the greatest variance between the quoted rates and my own calculations appear. Who knows? Maybe they push the envelope to intentionally make their rates look lower? Either way, I use this kind of calculation to guide where we might borrow and as you can guess I'm sure, I would rather pay my estimated 10.4% to Zopa than 19.4% to a Bank or 264% to Log Book Loans.

So for us **we rely on the asterisked Column J** figures – here Log Book Loans are still coming out as 13 times more expensive than the Bank and Sunny 18 times more expensive. They'd probably be happier with my numbers than the APRs!

- However hard up we were **I would never borrow from any lender above 30%,** I would sell assets off to fund a crisis, take a part-time job, anything instead – and all because of the impact of cumulative interest.

If this is all still too confusing, just pick a lender with the lowest percentage and lowest total amount to be repaid and borrow as little as you can! And then pay it off as quickly as you can.

> **Editors note**: I see what you've done here, all the loans quote different examples and loan periods making it hard to compare Annual rates, so you are working out a loosely comparable calculation of interest paid per month?

And then based on the amount borrowed work out a monthly interest rate, and times it by 12 for a sort of annual equivalent. But why have you doubled it?

> **Author's note** – I divided it by 0.5 (so in effect that doubles it) on the assumption that over the year only half the debt remains outstanding, so by definition that doubles the annual % rate. Good spot though.

Chapter 11
Arbitrage & Cakes

My last word on interest rates for a while involves **Arbitrage** – which apparently means in economics and finance, "The practice of taking advantage of a price difference between two or more markets: striking a combination of matching deals that capitalize upon the imbalance." You may have heard of sports arbitrage betting which is where you bet on both teams at different times when the odds change, meaning, in theory, that you can't lose – but I gather you can, for example if an event gets cancelled. It's the same as covering every square on a roulette table only to see Zero come in as the winning number and you lose!

Anyway, I had realised that as I had a good credit rating I could borrow money cheaply from a Bank or Zopa, at around 3.5% APR, so probably around a real rate of 1.7% per annum. And in theory at least I could lend it out to people with a less advantageous credit rate, via Zopa again (so I would unusually be both a borrower and saver/lender), at around 12% APR, so using my theory presumably a 6% real rate.

It wasn't as unethical as it sounds as my borrowers (Zopa split your savings into chunks and lend it out for you) needed money from somewhere and at least this way could borrow more cheaply than from a Bank or a Pay Day lender.

After allowing 2% for charges and loans that didn't get repaid that would mean I could arbitrage the money and make 6% net return on my money. For example 6% - 1.7% = 4.3%, - 2% = 2.3% for seemingly **doing nothing.** So after tax that would be a profit of around 1.75% by lending out money that I hadn't even had to earn or save myself. It's not a huge return but on say a loan of £25,000 over 8 years, that could add £3,500 to our wealth if my maths are correct or almost **£35 a month of free money**. Its enough to take Mrs R out for a bun and coffee, so I had to try it.

> **Editor's note** – Did it work out?

FACT 19. – *Yes, You can make money with other people's money!*

> **Author's note** – it worked exactly as planned, the true return was probably nearer £30 a month of free money. But in the end I cleared the debt years early – I simply didn't like owing anything to anyone plus I wasn't comfortable with the thought that we were taking on risk, for example if we had a sudden deep recession then bad debts would climb and we'd end up losing money each month. It wasn't worth continuing for 8 years just to prove a point.
>
> **Mrs R note** – I wondered why you stopped offering to take me out!
>
> **Author's note** – Sorry, now you know.

OK, I think that's more than enough about the power of accumulating money through investment or as a debt being a potential millstone around your neck.

Chapter 12

How Did We Spend and Make Money?

If you recall I said we've earned circa £1m and spent almost the same, but where exactly did we spend it and where did we save it to make our money?

> **Editor's note** - Why is this important?
>
> **Author's note** – Well if we stick with a Mars Bar analogy it seems obvious to me that if we have earnt say 100 Mars Bars in our lives and ate 80 Bars, then what we did with the missing 20 Bars must be pretty significant if we've ended up with 300 Mars Bars left now!
>
> **Editor's note** – OK, I get it, plus of course there is the issue of whether the 80 Mars Bars you ate is enough for a normal family to live on!
>
> But if I may say so I think that's enough of the Mars Bars analogies for a while too!
>
> **Author's note –** Agreed so let's put some meat on the bones so readers can get a feel for how our spending and savings patterns might compare to their own circumstances?

Where have we Spent Our Money?

The Table that follows is an approximate breakdown of how we spent or invested our joint wages, after tax, based on an **average years** earnings.

Table 8

TABLE 8	How We Spent our Money		Proportion
Running a Home	£	11,341	33%
Home Purchase	£	9,966	29%
Food/Clothes/Health	£	3,437	10%
Cars/Fuel/Transport	£	3,093	9%
Leisure/Fun/Phones	£	1,375	4%
Gifts & Charity	£	1,031	3%
Businesses	£	344	1%
Extra Tax Due outside PAYE	£	687	2%
Saving/Investment/Pensions	£	3,093	9%

Or if you are a picture person, see the chart that follows:

HOW WE SPENT EACH YEAR

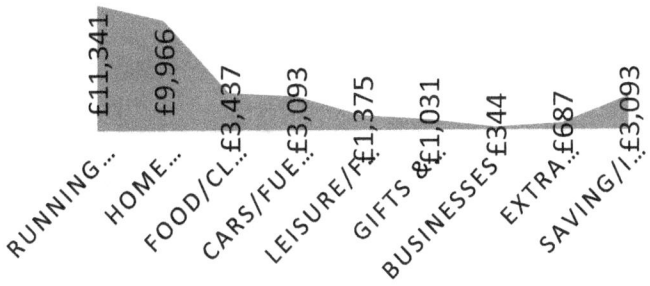

As you can see the costs of **running** a home (so that's furnishings, heating, lighting, council tax, insurance and so on) surprisingly outweighed the cost of **acquiring** it in the first place, even after allowing for moving home several times and paying mortgage interest, legal and removal fees.

> **Editor's note** – I always thought my own energy bills were too high!

> **Author's note** – Yep I'm afraid so. What I would term the essential utilities added up to about 15% of total income!

What was also interesting to me is that even without huge commuting costs, our total **transport costs are high**, so after including buying cars, fuel and insurance plus the odd train ticket they still came in as much as all our food, clothing and health costs (I'm not including National Insurance contributions here) combined. It surprised me.

- I think the Editor mentioned earlier in the Mars section (which I promised not to talk about again so don't tell him) that even though it seems ever more costly each passing year, in real terms food gets cheaper as production and storage techniques get more efficient every year, so maybe cars are more expensive than they seem?.

As you might imagine anyone who enjoys building a 40 year archive of financial records is probably **not a big spender on fun** or things like having a new posh mobile phone or laptop every year and we have in fact almost spent as much on other people, (for example for birthdays and Christmas) plus donations to charities than we have on these fun things. Over the whole period these latter payments to charities have tended to average around 1% of salary and currently stand at about 3%, so we could do more, but I'm at least pleased it's always been a tad bit better than the 0.7% of GDP the UK government aims to give to overseas aid each year, and we've tried to keep giving something even when we were hard up.

The last three columns in the graph have been grouped together on purpose as they represent where we spent the money that wasn't a part of our daily living, in effect this was our investment for the future and added up to around 12% of post-tax income over the years.

> NB. Other figures could be included here, such as costs paid on Buy to Let properties but that will just cloud the story, I will come onto that later in the book as for now I am just looking at how we have spent money in comparison to earnings, not how we have spent our gains to add yet more wealth..

So I think you could conclude that how we have made our money is a **combination of where we put this 12% plus of course how we saved money in the other 88%** to free up as much investment capital as possible. Before I explore that, let's look at the 12% in a bit more detail.

Chapter 13

Where We Invested

We have invested around **1% of our money in new businesses**, so that is either backing our own Ideas, backing other people or in get-rich-quick (in theory) schemes like Multi Level Marketing and various others programmes. You know the kind of thing, schemes you see every week on the Internet or in Direct Mail, I don't fall for many but I am a sucker for signing up to learn new skills. I will also talk about these kind of schemes later in more depth for you.

You will see that we have ear-marked an extra 2% for tax due outside PAYE (paid from income each month) so this covers things like extra tax on investments, capital gains on the sales of assets or shares, stamp duty of property acquisition for example.

Finally we have around **9% of income has been put aside into investments, savings and pensions.** Table 9 below brings everything together for you, with returns.

TABLE 9	Amount £	% of Investments	Value Achieved £	Growth	Return PA %
Contributory Pensions	£ 155,727	74%	£ 248,387	£ 92,660	5.4%
Investments	£ 35,250	17%	£ 74,000	£ 38,750	25.0%
Businesses	£ 15,000	7%	£ 1,364,924	£ 1,349,924	529.4%
MLM & Other Schemes	£ 5,000	2%	£ 2,000	-£ 3,000	-12.0%
Non-Con Final Salary Pension	£ 2,585	1%	£ 214,213	£ 211,628	263.4%

As the name suggest, contributory pensions are those we have chosen **voluntarily** to invest in (these have earned us around 5.4% per annum return versus an average Base Rate of 6.4%, so hardly stellar performance from professional managers!), whereas at the foot of Table 9 is the non-contributory pension where money was mostly paid in all by the employer to earn a pension in retirement that is a fixed proportion of final salary. Sadly these schemes are largely **extinct** these days, not surprisingly given the healthy return for the recipient, in this case, me, and this is now why the government doesn't encourage Financial Advisors to mess with these kinds of investments. So it's very rare these days to find a company or even government department offering this kind of deal as part of a salary package, if you see one somewhere like the NHS, Police or Department of Education, probably best to grab it!

Investments of various types (managed mostly by me) have performed well, generally **better than the inflation** rate and better than professional managers, so money invested here doubled roughly every 3 years.

And before I jump on to the star performer, lets talk a moment about so called **Get Rich Quick Schemes**. As you can see these did lose money but the overall position is perhaps not so bleak. They didn't lose money because they are scams as most people think, (it's actually a tightly regulated market in the UK) they lost money due to:

- Business Closure / Sale
- My inability to stick to the Training Plan
- Trying to Reinvent the Wheel
- Lack of Time Investment

With a partner, we estimated that well run MLM schemes will make you roughly **£1 per hour invested** provided you follow the plan. This isn't a lot versus the Average Wage, but if you stick at it and follow the plan, this £1 per hour per month can be **paid for life**. Invest 2,000 hours properly and you might just get back the equivalent to a £24,000 a year pension, so it shouldn't be dismissed.

Our small return wasn't from such profits but the tax savings from running a second business against which certain expenses can be offset. Plus we should not discount the value of lessons learned which may have unwittingly delivered benefits in my efforts in real business, the star performer being the significant profits made in this area.

Investments in various **businesses which total around £15,000 in hard cash have ended up creating wealth of around £1.2m** so whilst that's only around the same as all the salaries added together over the years, the reality is better and lessons can be learnt from this money too.

We invested the proceeds of selling businesses in shares and property with the following additional beneficial results:

	£Investment	£Value Now	£Plus Net Income	£Growth
Buy To Let Property	1,089,865	1,410,000	134,722	454,857
Shares	97,920	160,250		62,750

> NB. Whilst the shares have performed particularly well (the actual return is even better than shown but confusing to explain in any more detail as these are shares on the UK AIM junior stock market) so I do not feel the return is necessarily duplicatable, but I am showing it for completeness.

With regard to the business investments themselves, I have tried to pick a **variety** of different approaches, in effect, having more than one horse in the race. Many ideas haven't even got off the drawing board but of course that also means they won't have wasted a lot of money, and in many cases these costs may still be **tax deductible** as the government wants to encourage innovation and may even pay you more than you spent! The message really is that even a failure isn't a failure, the best tip is to keep on trying.

So we have been involved in **manufacture, wholesaling, retail, internet trading** (with stock), internet drop-shipping (someone else sends it for you), via Amazon, plus **agency / services** businesses. Plus of course all the aforementioned Multi-Level Marketing schemes. In summary, I may have been involved in 40 business ideas **(so roughly one new business per year),** and of these circa 25% make it through to a proper trading status, a couple have lost relatively small amounts of money, most have broken even or made a small profit, and a couple have been big successes. But you only need one decent success to transform your families fortunes.

FACT 20. – *Maybe not for everyone but spreading our risk widely gave us enough breadth of businesses that something was bound to work!*

I suppose the moral here is it doesn't matter what you try, **the key is to do something, keep the risk to a minimum** and try and pick things you might reasonably enjoy or at least have some detailed knowledge about rather than picking at random.

Our trading business that I can remember looked like this.

Table 10

TABLE 10.	Started	Years	Investment	Return PA
Netcallidus/S4 (Agency)	2000	10	£ 37,500	157%
Ride On Toy Cars (Internet)	2009	7	£ 3,600	4%
Crave Maternity Clothing (Manufacture)	2010	2	£ 14,000	4%
Seriously Helpful (Agency)	2012	6	£ 5,000	215%
Stunning Jewellery (Drop Ship)	2013	3	£ 3,600	6%
Interwebbing (Software)	2014	4	£ 12,292	-43%
Innovative world (Amazon)	2015	3	£ 10,209	-20%
Average		5	£ 12,314	46%

We set out with the goal to **just beat normal investment returns** (say 5% overall) and as you can see with the averages at the foot of Table 10, overall, businesses have performed about 8x better than professional investments like pensions and also beaten property growth – and this assumes that we extract no value whatsoever from recent new ventures started in the last few years and which are currently in loss. If we removed the last two entries from the table then the average annual return jumps to over **75% per annum.**

- Interestingly our latest agency is more successful than the first we started a decade earlier despite tougher markets which probably also goes to show that you do **learn how to do things better** and differently the more you practice. Our results have been **strongest where we have started a business from scratch** rather than acquired somebody else's baby and tried to improve it!

Aside from the business side of things, the real star of our portfolio has also been the decision to invest business sale proceeds into **property investment** where on average over 3 years we have made about **10% per annum growth** in property value plus around **4% in income**, that's almost 14% after all costs and taxes are paid. Now of course just like interest rates property prices go up and down over time and as an investment class it has the added complication of regional variances too, so repetition of results certainly can't be relied upon. But to me it's interesting to see that **just looking at net income from rentals, investment property has performed almost as well as professionally managed investments** such as pensions and surely people will always want to rent houses?

In summary, we regard the growth in the value of our properties as a bonus but it serves to prove the old adage that when you have money, its easier to make more and I think this can generally be applied to savings. With savings, you can make more and overall enjoy more things in life whereas **borrowing reduces the things you get to do as you are making somebody else rich** – that could be a Bank, Money Lender, shareholder or landlord.

The trick of course is having the discipline to save money when you can, and even if you can't find business ideas to invest in, it still makes sense to squirrel money away so it is working for you every day by growing.

Chapter 13

Let's Break Down the Investments in More Detail

Over the years we have tried many different things but they can probably be broadly categorised as follows:

		Average Investment		Profit	Return PA %
TABLE 11					
SAYE Shares	£	16,980	£	18,046	10.4%
National Savings	£	1,000	£	750	5.8%
Share Day-Trading	£	9,827	£	105	5.5%
Profit Share Bonuses	£	11,123	£	1,287	2.3%
Managed Investment Bonds	£	12,600	£	786	0.1%
Hot tips	£	1,373	-£	1,210	-39.2%

I have ranked them in as you will see in order of the best annual performance overall so lets talk about them individually.

Save As You Earn (SAYE)

FACT 21. – *Probably the nearest you'll ever get to betting on a SURE thing*

SAYE schemes are shares generally awarded to employees of larger companies as a perk and they impact the employees of around 1,000 companies and **5% of the UK workforce**, but increasingly smaller companies are copying the idea as a way to keep staff loyal.

In these schemes you generally have to pay for the shares yourself by **salary sacrifice** each month from your wages and the best kept secret about these schemes is that the price you might chose to buy at isn't the price of the shares in a few years' time, but today's price, and if it worsens you don't need to proceed. So it's literally like entering a casino and being allowed the privilege of leaving your chips on the roulette table if a winning number comes up and sneaking them off it's a losing number. Only the casino owner gets privileges like that!

So to clarify the price you can buy shares in future for is fixed today but the deal isn't agreed until the shares become due in a few years' time, by which point your monthly savings will have added up to the planned purchase price. Schemes vary as regulations change but when I did these we also received a modest interest rate or bonus, often 10%, on the money put aside, plus I saved the tax on the money I willingly sacrificed from my salary (and provided you buy the shares and keep them for a while, they remain tax free). Then, come the day of allotment, you get a **choice**. If the shares have fallen in value, you can simply have your **cash back plus interest** minus a bit of tax. So that's still usually better off than taking the cash with your salary as you have in effect been investing tax free money cumulatively.

But what if the share price has gone up in the years you've been saving – from memory its usually 3 or 5 years? Your shares might have been allocated to you at **say £0.10** each and they are now worth **£1.00** each, so you will have more than multiplied your money by 10 times or **1,000%** and you'll also be able to use the interest earned to buy shares at £0.10 too.

I was put onto this wonderful opportunity by a wealthy Director of HSBC and have availed myself of it ever since – as you can see the average annual returns of **10.4%** for my past schemes almost doubled the success of my pensions and its completely risk free as far as I can work out.

> NB. And this is after deducting what we would have made if we'd invested in the money in a decent savings account, so it's real extra profit.

Sadly, due to circumstances (things like moving house, starting a family) I only managed to subscribe for 40% of my maximum entitlement during the time I was at work – which means I let £26,000 of guaranteed profit go to waste. You can't win them all of course, we did still make a respectable extra £18,000 profit, tax free.

National Savings

FACT 22. – *Worth consideration as the rates are OK and it should be safe.*

Here I include any government sponsored Bonds that pay a guaranteed amount above inflation in interest, or a fixed rate, each year plus Premium Bonds with the chance to win a big prize in lieu of interest (but you can still work out an approximate rate of interest based on the size of prize fund and probability of winning. Unless you are a lucky person these pay less equivalent interest, as prizes, than if you'd invested in other government backed savings products).

Any winnings I had have been factored in to arrive at the overall real return after tax. As you can see 5.8% compares **favourably** with other investments we have made (but will be time dependent, for example it will pay more if it was taken out when interest rates were high and the costs for the government to borrow money anywhere else would also be high) and in general I would say these are competitive products and generally tax free. I suppose they are as safe as the UK economy – if that goes bust we all have more than our Premium Bonds to worry about!

Share Day-Trading

FACT 23 – *Great fun and easier than working, but very high risk*

I may not be using this term in its correct literal sense as it purports to represent a class of investors who buy securities during the day and **always sell them** (or the reverse) by the close of play that same day. In my own case I employ a mix of Day Trading and a different strategy called Buy and Hold to create a hybrid strategy. A Buy and Hold investor is a speculator who hold stocks for the **long-term** in the assumption that over many years, markets generally rise, so the value of shares rises too.

What I do is identify in advance stocks and shares I like the look of, **wait** for a price decline which I perceive to be a blip rather than part of a broader decline (so I will be looking for **profitable** companies with a good basis of sound **assets**), I then enter the market with a view to a Day Trade type exit by the close of play (in practice as soon as I have made any decent profit) but if said profit is not forthcoming I will HOLD until hell freezes over and I either eventually make a profit, after deducting all costs, or the offending company and shares go bust!

So for me a suitable **gain might be only £10** after costs. On principle I don't close out with even a penny loss at the end of the day as my strategy is to hold onto the shares forever until they make an eventual profit! This even includes making an allowance for any lost interest I could have earned if I hadn't bought the shares, and profits include any dividends paid to me whilst I hold them.

If the stock keeps dropping I may go back into the market and buy again, thereby lowering the average price paid (this is also my own variant on a technique called Least Cost Averaging) and whilst it makes sense mathematically it has to be said that doubling up like this massively increases risk.

> **Editor's Note** - I didn't think you were in favour of doubling up – Isn't that the same as the unaffordable chess-board scenario described earlier? PS. Did you know that Keynes said that stock markets were just expensive casinos? I've always found it amusing that the word stockbroker neatly hides the word broke!
>
> **Author's note** – You are absolutely correct. I generally invest in £2,000 chunks so if my first deal goes badly, I would double up to £4,000 (assuming I had the funds spare), but if it continued to drop I wouldn't go to £8,000 but £6,000. In effect then it's closer to the idea of putting pennies in a box, going up one penny at a time but I'm using £2,000 as my preferred unit, not one penny.

PS. I remember my old business partner telling me about an old betting system called the **Martingale** that isn't so different in principle. It's a guaranteed win (unless you run out of cash, just like the Emperor would run out of grain) hence most gambling establishments prevent you from increasing your stake like this for long, usually by implementing a maximum bet size.

Having previously always bought shares for the long term, held them for years and checked progress rarely, I had always thought that was the best approach, until a millionaire friend told me of his approach of even taking small profits on the basis of ***a bird in the hand is worth two in the bush***. I copied him, developed my own spin on his technique and have used it very successfully for almost two decades, and in fact recently made **£2,050 profit on a £19,900 investment in just 6 weeks,** which after deducting what I could have earned more safely in interest instead. still amounts to about 84% per annum return, if I could repeat the trick ten times a year!

It's obviously significantly better than our overall performance in pensions and a lot more fun than working for a month for a similar return. It is even better when you consider the additional fact that this took **minutes**, as I do not sit slavishly watching stock prices all day. Most days I forget to check more than once.

However, this was an unusual transaction (the average **gain is nearer £105 on a £9,800 stake/investment**) and in studying my many years of trades for this book, I have learnt some important extra facts which have surprised me:

- Obviously this is **high risk** – you can lose all your money so I should really only invest what we can afford to lose, not the home improvement budget (see below) and I won't be doing that again.
- That said it's probably not as high risk as gambling at the casino or on horses – as with my strategy you keep your money in the game **forever** until you get a winning exit, or the share goes bust.
- The overall return of 5.5% after tax and opportunity cost (lost interest) is not so different from my pension performance. It's just more fun and more stress!
- As going bust is a rare event, but does happen, it's important **to have more than one horse (**asset) in the race. But in most cases it seems to me to be the equivalent of betting on a race and being allowed to keep your horse running forever, until it wins!

So as I have said my goal is to sell quickly, in a day if possibly but failing that I aim generally for within a week. But have been known to hold a share for 18 months (after it fell 90%)

just to be stubborn and get my money back. I actually ended up making a modest 3% profit but had lost 5% in missed interest earnings.

> **Editor's note** – I remember Mrs H telling me you made this investment with all your savings to make a profit for a new conservatory?
>
> **Author's note** – Correct, I bet she didn't mention her insistence that we sell the shares immediately (after they'd plummeted) to salvage the 10% of value left? Obviously with my long term *keep-it-forever* plan, I ignored that idea and just delayed building the conservatory. It came good in the end as we got all our money back and only lost a bit of interest we could have had. Its lucky we didn't have any other calls on our money with broken cars for example in that 18 months and I learned a valuable lesson anyway. Nearly an expensive lesson.
>
> **Editor's Note** – Yes, I remember. You said you thought the stock markets were an example of a Perfect Information / Perfect Competition whereby everything about a stock is publicly shared to those who buy it and everyone has an equal chance to trade so if you do your research, you should be fairly safe. Whereas in practice you discovered that secret *behind-closed-doors* deals can happen after the markets are shut to the general public, and in this case, your target share, which shall remain nameless (in case we are unfairly chastising them) sold off a big chunk of their business privately, thereby spooking the markets and cutting 90% off the share value upon the stock re-opening the next morning. So the

> shares weren't dropping on sentiment. They had already dropped whilst the markets were shut, decimating your investment value. It could have been nasty.
>
> **Author's note** – I agree, it re-affirms the point: if you do invest, assume you might lose it all, and expect the worst so don't get over confident. In recent years I have refined my strategy so I tend to only gamble with my winnings. I've safely removed my original seed money. I still don't want to lose what's left though.

If you are interested in this kind of **gambling**, because that's probably what it's best truly described as, then I have concluded it is also necessary to find stocks which **regularly change value** more than the spread (profit margin) charged by the City Brokers (so that is the difference between the buying and selling price) plus you have to add on a small buying and selling fee and a special stock-market tax. On my size of deal fees generally add up to about £30 to buy and sell (you also need to remember to pay tax on your gains, less any annual allowances). For me, in the UK, this meant I tended to try and find shares with **regular price movement in the day of around 3%.**

> NB. As I trade shares regularly, with brokers like **JS Bell** or **Hargreaves Lansdown** it is possible to get **reduced fees if you deal 2/3 times a week**. This is easy to achieve if you are buying and selling quickly – the fees then drop to around **£20** in total on a buy and sell, but I work on the higher figure to give myself an edge with an extra £10 pure profit.

Most recently, assuming the worst with Brexit, I have invested in companies that also **pay dividends above 5%,** so if the worst comes to the worst and the stock plummets,

I should still get a decent income. So that's led to energy companies like SSE but please don't just copy me! In my head I had previously worked out that with a £300,000 fund split across 30 different business in a mix of trades (so that when one sector declines another hopefully booms) then my style of day trading could reliably make about £3,000 per month income. In effect, enough to give up the day job and again substantially better than the £1,000-£2,000 a month most pensions might yield. In practice as Table 11 confirms the overall returns weren't that great but nevertheless I still estimate with a fund of around **£400,000** and a £50,000 emergency pot it should be possible to match the UK average wage, after tax, by share trading. Many people's pension fund will exceed this, but it's certainly not for the faint hearted and not necessarily money you should gamble with.

Whilst it's a lot more fun day trading than working in the office or buying National Savings products, it is of course much more risky. And with hindsight, even though I still make on average around **£15 per day profit from my version of day trading** in just 5 minutes per day, I've learnt about the real risk of losing everything so probably will now **stop and invest my efforts more sensibly** and safely into new business ideas instead!

What else has the analysis about share trading taught me?

- I learnt that it is getting **tougher to make a return by about 1% per annum** – I assume this is as a result of general market forces and pessimism or the fact that electronic systems keep levelling the playing field?
- And very surprisingly I have realised, again with hindsight, that **I made more money from companies I know less about**, in a ratio around 3:1. I had assumed

companies where I had fairly deep strategic knowledge, such as the banks I worked in or the company I sold my business to would equate to better results as I'd have an intuitive feel as to when to buy and sell. In practice the opposite seems to be true, just like increasing investment amounts (or increasing stakes in a game of cards) alters your behaviour without it being apparent, I think the same is true here and knowledge makes you panic and delay some actions and speed up others. So for every **£105 I made in companies I know well, I made almost £300 in what I termed "stranger" companies.** Isn't life weird and wonderful!

- I have discovered that in the shares I mostly trade (TelecomPlus, DotDigital, SSE, Barclays) I can sometimes do well **two or three times in the same day** as its often easiest to make a quick profit **as soon as the markets open**, again around **lunchtime** and then sometimes just as the markets are **about to close** in mid-afternoon. So you could in theory buy and sell the same shares and profit three times in a day. And even with small £10-£15 profits each time this can easily add up to a **huge annualised rate of return**, potentially 200-300% pa. More so if you kept growing your investment size to take account of the aforementioned Einstein cumulative rule, but I don't do that or have all my eggs in any one basket – I always have and always will like to spread risk across a growing portfolio of shares and other investments.

I will jump ahead for a minute as Hot Tips are another kind of share trading, albeit with the intention of holding shares for longer, typically in new companies. You can see the results for Hot Tips at the foot of Table 11, it's not a pretty picture.

Hot Tips

FACT 24. – *Someone benefits from Tips, it probably won't be you!*

By this I don't think I mean illegal insider trading but strong recommendations to buy from friends, family, brokers, bankers, lawyers for example – anyone who has close knowledge of a company and its big deals.

This was our worst performing asset class **losing almost 90% of the money invested** and equating to an annual loss of almost 40% as it generally took a few years to go down the pan. What I concluded is that the City is mostly a rigged game and you need to know the rules – so in just the same way that we nearly lost the family shirt and conservatory from an after-hours deal, this is another example.

What I think happens is that city advisors working on deals plus the founders in companies get preferential deals on shares as **they are in at the start** for pennies on the pound. They then talk up the game to successive investors by which time the sale price has accumulated, say to a pound. By the time you get a tip, it's simply too late, the horse has bolted even if they weren't intentionally trying to fleece you. The original sellers cash in a few more share options, the price drops, and you can be left as the muppet that unwittingly overpaid.

The moral of the story is easy – **never believe in tips from any source!**

> PS. A late addition to the book, I have recently had a very small ($200) dabble in the Bit Coin type market which is all the rage with pundits – and guess what, true to form it's currently losing money, not a lot but it proves the point of this section of the book!

Profit Sharing

FACT 25. – *It's like getting cash from the ATM at 10% off*

This is a type of investment or saving that is related a bit to SAYE schemes as it is mostly an opportunity for employees in large companies, but it may be available in smaller ones too. In essence, the company declares an annual profit, decide to share some of this with staff in say the Summer or at Christmas time, and they give you the **option** of having cash, shares, or a combination.

Obviously cash is tempting and taken by most but as you would expect, as this is, in effect, extra income, it is generally all taxed at your highest rate of income tax and you probably pay National Insurance too. So for most people you **lose at least £0.35** out of every pound before you even think of treating yourself!

Conversely, just like SAYE, shares will often be free of all taxes provided you hold them for a period. In Table 11 you will see that I estimate a poor return of just 2.3% per annum (after taking account of what I could have done with the money had I accepted cash) but this doesn't tell the full story – my experience of these schemes was solely when interest rates were very high so we lost a lot of interest and it's skewed the results a bit I think.

On further reflection and calculation I have concluded that:

- Taking Profit Sharing as shares instead of cash was equivalent to adding 3% to my annual pay
- Every £1 taken as cash effectively cost about £1.55 whereas if I had taken shares instead (and cashed them later) every £1 would then only have cost me about £0.90.

Who doesn't like money when its available in a 10% OFF sale?...**even better if its 40% off** which is the equivalent cost of 90 pence versus £1.55

Again due to family circumstances it appears that I managed to have the discipline to stick to shares instead of cash to the extent of about **40% of my maximum potential**, so not bad, but I know I could have been more disciplined.

Managed Investment Bonds

This is a class of investment where I have trusted my money to professional money managers. Now I'm sorry, I know my percentage won't agree with anything you'll read in the press and I must just have bad luck picking funds or managers or whatever it was, but with just 0.1% gain they did well to give me my money back. No doubt a few fat fees were taken out along the way by advisors.

> **Editor's note** – Did you know that it's not uncommon to pay an advisor 1-2% of a fund value for a single bit of financial advice that might take just a few hours? That's often £5,000 commission taken out of your hard earned money. I know they need to make a living too and have expensive research services to maintain, but honestly £5k.
>
> **Author's note** – Don't remind me. I discovered that kind of fee in the small print of a product I'd taken out not so long ago. I wanted to pay into a pension for just a couple of years (to get the tax advantages of about £8,000), so I pretty much prescribed to them exactly what I wanted, right down to the supplier. Imagine my surprise when I discovered they'd made almost as much for a half hour meeting as I did by sacrificing a large chunk of my pay for a couple of years! I only discovered this

gem when researching the paperwork in more detail to help with the research for this book, so thanks for ruining my day!

Any more Learning from the research?

Yes, I have learnt something I didn't quite expect from about every area of spend or investment we've made, so let's look at a few in more detail. Let's start with:

Buying a Home

We bought our first home at quite an early age (early 20s) and in the initial years moved every **50 months** or so as we climbed up the property ladder. We have stayed in our last house, the most expensive, for over 20 years and overall our occupancy in each home averages around **nine years**, which isn't far off the UK average which until recently was around seven years. This has been getting longer of late as people choose to improve not move, probably mostly to avoid all the agents and lawyers' fees, plus taxes which get ever more onerous.

By moving up the ladder and arriving in our most expensive house it is easy to conclude that this is a good idea as plainly we have **made the most profit on the last house**, partially because we have lived there the longest, and secondly, in pure cash terms, it is the most expensive to start with so any gains will obviously be greater in money terms, if not percentages.

Further investigation shows a more complex picture. In Table 12.1 below I have listed each type of house transaction in the **order in which it happened**, so our first house was a pre-war semi-detached, then a very narrow, new, detached (circa 1,000 square feet so it should probably have been called a detached terrace!), then a traditional 1970s sized detached (probably 2,000 square feet) and then our most recent house, a large new detached, circa 3,500 square feet with quarter acre gardens or thereabouts.

Table 12.1

TABLE 12.1	Type	Years	Profit	Profit PA	Real Profit	Average Base Rate	House Prices	Difference	Result?
1	Semi	3	£ 3,500	10%	-£2,370	16.7%	6.5%	10.2%	Bad
2	Small Detached	5	£ 26,000	28%	£13,975	13.6%	11.8%	1.8%	Great
3	Normal Detached	8	£ 5,500	1%	-£71,229	12.4%	2.4%	10.0%	Terrible
4	Large Detached	22	£ 418,000	12%	£258,958	6.3%	6.9%	-0.6%	Good?

I have then shown how long we owned the property, the profit after sale (excluding legal costs), and from this, estimated an annual profit percentage.

- So as you can see highlighted the small detached was a star performer, presumably as we got a good deal from a builder. But in absolute scale of profit, the largest and last property has brought in the most money, but not per annum.

The **real profit** is how much has been made **after taking account of the cost of funds**, so that means what we could have done if instead of stretching ourselves, we had instead invested our equity that we were putting into the larger property (as deposit) into a high interest savings account – so instead of a bigger home we would have earned money on our savings.

Finally for my own information I listed out the average Base Rate during the tenancy period, the Average House Price Inflation rate for the same period (taken from Nationwide Building Society data) and then measured the difference. I found this illuminating.

In Table 12.2 that follows I have then **simply re-ordered the houses by the seemingly best performing profit margin** (I am treating the Home here as just another investment, not a lifestyle decision for example) and, interestingly, **this revealed, to me at least, a trend in the Difference Column** when compared to the Result, that is whether it was a good or bad decision to move.

I don't know whether I suspected this trend **subconsciously** or indeed if it has any real merit amongst property experts but something was going on as we certainly seem to have generally timed our moves fairly well.

So in Table 12.3 I have then listed the properties in decreasing order of said Difference Column.

So for me this seems like an obvious but **Little Known Secret about property**?

I've then added in a row for rates today for comparison purposes!

Table 12.2 and Table 12.3

TABLE 12.2	Type	Years	Profit	Profit PA	Real Profit	Average Base Rate	House Prices	Difference	Result
3	Normal Detached	8	£ 5,500	1%	-£71,229	12.4%	2.4%	10.0%	Terrible
1	Semi	3	£ 3,500	10%	-£ 2,370	16.7%	6.5%	10.2%	Bad
4	Large Detached	22	£ 418,000	12%	£258,958	6.3%	6.9%	-0.6%	Good?
2	Small Detached	5	£ 26,000	28%	£13,975	13.6%	11.8%	1.8%	Great

TABLE 12.3	Type	Years	Profit	Profit PA	Real Profit	Average Base Rate	House Prices	Difference	Result
3	Normal Detached	8	£ 5,500	1%	-£ 71,229	12.4%	2.4%	10.0%	Terrible
1	Semi	3	£ 3,500	10%	-£2,370	16.7%	6.5%	10.2%	Bad
2	Small Detached	5	£ 26,000	28%	£13,975	13.6%	11.8%	1.8%	Great
4	Large Detached	22	£ 418,000	12%	£ 258,958	6.3%	6.9%	-0.6%	Good?
TODAY						0.6%	2.0%	-1.4%	Who Knows?

So what is my conclusion from all this?

FACT 25. – *(Or is it FICTION?) – Best to buy when the difference in rates is low.*

After allowing for lost interest earnings, and with the benefit of hindsight, it appears in real terms we lost money on two of our four properties but luckily have made up more than the difference elsewhere.

The best returns seem to have occurred when the differences between Base Rate (which has a correlation on the mortgage rate) and the rate of house price inflation are the smallest or negative. I suppose in simple terms that's like saying you are not subsidizing your house by paying too much for the money unless the house is going up in value faster. The times when our home purchases did worst, looking back, were when we had to buy or when the market was in a panic with prices rising rapidly.

Closer inspection of the data revealed that using this as a guide, across the last 40 or so years there have clearly been times when it might have been better to buy than not. On average **we purchased within about 12 months of the sweet spot**, and presumably this is why (ignoring lost interest) all our properties have made some profit – we have never had negative equity.

Obviously I'm not a financial advisor or housing specialist, so what do I know? (So please don't just transfer my possibly flawed conclusion into your own behaviour without research – but what do you conclude from these tables yourself?)

But all this post-event data suggests to me now is a possibly **opportune time to buy** as houses are only rising nationally (in June 2018) at around 2% per annum and you can borrow mortgages at around 3.5%, so you are losing out to the extent of only about 1.5% subsidy to get on the ladder or upscale. This seems a lot less risky than the 10+ subsidy we were making on our two badly performing properties.

> NB. With property prices dropping slightly in some areas at the moment and mortgage rates still being low (or at least not going up much) it may still be sensible to wait a while, but potentially the market is good to buy now according to our past examples.

I have promised not to talk again about how interest and mortgages work but safe to say, its worth shopping around for a good deal and keeping the loan period as short as sensibly possible.

- I did think we may have been helped along by the so-called "Cheap Staff Mortgage" that Bank and Building

Society staff are supposed to benefit from. Actually our staff mortgage rate averaged around 5.5% when the average Base Rate was almost the same at 5.4% so our employers didn't help so much after all. Maybe 1% benefit there, but not what you'd expect, plus I think we got taxed on it anyway!

What about saving money on the costs of moving and or buying a house?

Obviously estate agents cost a pretty penny whoever you go with and it's certainly a good idea to negotiate reduced fees for things like a protracted sale. I remember we did this once and the agent failed to define what counted as a quick or slow sale, so needless to say they didn't get the maximum fee on that occasion – more-fool them!

Part of the total purchase disbursement costs are of course fixed by law, so things like Stamp Duty are fixed percentages and a number of legal processes like Local Authority Searches have fixed prices that can't be negotiated down, but you may not need every service offered by agents or lawyers and that's certainly one way we managed to save some money towards buying better houses over the years.

I don't think legal fees are worth skimping on just to save a few hundred pounds. Most conveyancers these days are a bit ropey and it's not surprising as the poor staff are hugely overworked yet charge less now than we paid 30 years ago. Being disappointed with the generally poor quality, we recently tried a **really cheap** lawyer to act for one of our buy-to-let purchases on the basis of *how bad can it be – if even good isn't great?*....turns out, **really bad**. Sure we saved £500 or so on fees but they were so bad at the job we were needlessly gazumped on a property and ended up spending **£3,000 more on the asking price**. We complained, got nowhere, so went to the legal ombudsman and won our case – but all you get awarded is a token compensation payment for poor service, not what you've lost or even a contribution towards it from the lawyer's indemnity insurers. We lost £3,000 and got back just £200, it wasn't worth the effort of complaining.

> **Editor's note** – it's not like you to lose money that easily?
>
> **Author's note** – Don't worry, luckily I had thought ahead and tested out the crazy plan of engaging Messrs Cheap, Rubbish & Rude on a property where we also owned most of the rest of the development. So even though we had to pay £3,000 more it's not wasted money as it in effect pushes up the apparent value of all homes in the area – so we lost £3,000 in hard cash but gained about £20,000 in the paper value of the rest of the properties there as future buyers will see that's what property in this area goes for.
>
> **Editor's note** – Unbelievable!

Anything else about property?

Yes, we've learnt that all the money spent on home furnishings over the years hasn't been a good investment. I know it's for personal enjoyment and ease of living too but an awful lot of people do seem to waste a huge amount of money in this area.

- Of the approximate **£85,000** we've spent in total on furnishings and the like, I estimate if we were to try and sell off our assets, these would raise at best around **£12,000**, so that's only 15p in the pound.

- By comparison of the **£296,000** spent acquiring the family home, it is today probably worth **double** that – so the house is a better investment. However that doubling of value has taken place over 40 years and across several properties (it's all our equity stakes added up). In terms of an annual percentage return it works out at about a return of **only 2.3%** per annum, after knocking off what our money could have earned us elsewhere that is…..so not as good as putting your money in an investment account, but on the upside we live there!
- If we compare that to investing in smaller properties which are then rented out as **Buy to Let** properties, even in these troubled Brexit days we have averaged around **13.9% per annum** return overall over the last 6 years.

I think my final word on property is actually two sentences. Don't ever be tempted to cut costs on **Insurance**, so read the small print and ensure you are adequately covered as insurers will only cover you pro-rata the cost of an event if your whole property isn't covered for the full amount.

FACT 26. – *It could take a lifetime to get back money lost by not being insured*

Let's give an example, you should really insure your home for £300,000 but you cut costs with a £200,000 policy in the belief (like my lawyer decision, *how bad can it be?*) the house would have to collapse to do that much damage. You end up having a flood that damages a couple of rooms badly and the costs are £30,000, so you'd assume you are covered as that's still under £200,000? Wrong, in many cases an insurer will say, "Your £200k is actually only two thirds of the £300k it should be, so we will pay two thirds of your £30,000 claim. Here is your cheque for £19,500 after we've deducted a £500 excess. So you saved £10 a month on the premium but are £10,500 down on the claim. It will take almost 100 years to get the money back at £10 a month!

FACT 27 or FICTION. – *If you regularly upsize, your last move may be one too many?*

The second thing I wanted to say is that given our learning about the rates of return on our home versus our investments, with hindsight we would probably have **stayed put one house move earlier**, that is in a smaller less expensive house and not moving into our current one, and instead put our spare resources into investment property. This would have two benefits: less need to downsize when you get older, plus income would grow for a more financially robust retirement. Whereas putting the cash into the family home is, in effect, leaving income on the table instead of in your pocket.

Automobiles

As you know already this is one of my favourite topics and I've even written a book or two about it, but whilst I don't calculate my fuel consumption every week or anything like that, I do have extensive records about my car purchases and have been able to conclude we have **probably paid about 40% less than most people, per mile**.

But how?

I have concluded the following:

- On average we paid £10,000 for each car versus the new cost of £21,000 so we were paying below 50% and always negotiated very hard.
- We've always invested (if that's the right word) in nice cars, not the kind of stinker you see Walter White drive in Breaking Bad, and I assume stinkers depreciate more

as nobody wants to own one. Cars were typically 3 years old when acquired so had lost 17.5% in value each year before we bought them!
- Even the lowest depreciating cars like Mercedes tend to lose around 12.5%, the worst almost 30% per annum, so we were buying at the better end of this league table.

    NB. Despite owning an Aston Martin (which does depreciate slowly and can even appreciate in value) over 40 or so years we have "invested" £108,000 in cars and if we sold them off today we would probably be left with just **30p in the Pound.** At first sight this doesn't seem great, although let's not forget we've used said investment to also drive circa 16 times around the planet.

    NB. These figures ignore three company cars so my research only covers the remaining 90% of privately funded motoring.

- We sold them on after a further 3.3 years for £5,250 so lost less per year in our ownership at 14.5% in value pa. So at the 6.3 year point when we generally sell our cars on they had in total lost 75% of their value. So as you can see our current asset value of 30p in the pound is pretty good, we've beat the general averages.
- On average we achieved car **depreciation of just £125 per month** – a lot less than any PCP deal. More about that particular scam in a minute!

How else can you save money when buying cars?

FACT 28. – *It's not the car itself that's the expensive bit!*

Aside from haggling and using real money, other good tips are to shop around for your **Car Insurance**. I have found that by using online services at different times of the day, premiums vary by as much as **10%** (this trick almost always seems to work best in the **early hours** of the morning). You can also add extra older drivers, real people of course, I'm not suggesting you make up imaginary folk!

I think the insurers must then assume (wrongly, as they don't bother to ask) that each driver does the same proportion of the mileage, so if you add a more experienced driver, the **average** price will reduce irrespective of whether they only set foot in the car once and drive a mile or drive it 50/50 with you. Adding too many drivers or those with bad records obviously increases the cost.

It's worth remembering too that the car running costs, so that's fuel, servicing, tyres, tax and insurance will be **far more expensive than the car itself.** Despite not doing huge mileages, **for every £1 net we spent on the car itself, we spent around £2.30** on all these other costs combined – so whilst I admit I've never picked a car on fuel economy or insurance group, this is worth evaluating. Next time we change cars I think I will see if we can reduce costs further by looking at cars with longer service intervals, better fuel economy, buying tyres that last for longer, cheaper insurance groups and so on. Sadly that may mean it's time for a boring car but at least it will cost less per mile, and come to think of it things like the Mitsubishi PHEV don't look half bad in the right colour!

- On the subject of tyres, in my experience cheap tyres may seem cheap but will generally need replacing more often, thereby incurring fitting, balancing and valve charges. The MPG is often slightly lower on cheaper rubber compounds and they wear less well, so I fit top of the range tyres as they are also generally safer. IMHO some things aren't worth scrimping on.

It's tempting of course to try and stick a car through a business but as best as I can work out, and I've tried checking this with the accountant but it is a complex area, all the tax advantages seem to now have been removed, in the UK at least. In my opinion it seems easiest to just bite the bullet and buy the car yourself out of taxed income. There are still opportunities to use a business to save costs though, for example, you might double up a work trip with pleasure – so you aren't having to carry 100% of the fuel costs yourself, subject to tax rules of course and it being a real justifiable journey.

I think we're done with cars other to add that contrary to what you might expect, routine servicing is often cheaper at main dealers than independent garages – but I have also recently started trialling mobile mechanics with good results so far both in terms of convenience and price.

Actually I've just realised we can't leave the car section without sharing my thoughts on the **latest car rental / purchase schemes.** I've been convinced for a while that these are akin to a scam, if only due to the plethora of car adverts on the television and the fact we buy more new cars per head in the UK than just about any comparable sized nation – plus these schemes are even migrating down to second hand vehicles. This wouldn't happen if it wasn't a good deal for someone, and I have a suspicion that's **not the consumer**.

So what have a I concluded?

FACT 29. – *Save money by buying the car yourself.*

All the PCP (**Personal Contract Plans**) I've looked at seem like they are a bit of sharp trading if not exactly a scam. It grieves me to see that the legislation that governs things like loans and the likes of Wonga has not woken up to the fact that car manufacturers and car finance brokers can advertise cars in a wholly misleading way by not revealing the true **TOTAL** cost.

Lets make up an example and see how true it rings to you:

> "Here is our **top of the range XYZ Sportster Turbo** – yours for just **£245 a month"** : Small print adds something like "Customer deposit £4950, Contract Purchase over 48 months, Final Option to Buy payment £12,000)

Looks like a really great deal? I get suckered in and almost order myself!

I believe (but can't prove) that many people in the UK think:

> "Gosh that's cheap...I earn £2,300 a month so that's only about **10% of my wages"** (on average wage).

> "I'm going to move up in the world with a posh car"

So they get themselves into a mess a few years down the road by paying for cars they really can't afford and shouldn't try to. This is why: few people have worked out the maths to calculate the real ownership cost and the government don't give us any guidance as car sales help keep the economy afloat even though most are imported!

> **Editor's note** – you might be onto something. I heard that Spain makes twice as many cars as the UK but purchases half as many new ones!

> **Author's note** – Yes, there has to be a good reason why in a slowdown the car companies are in our faces so much. I reckon every third TV advert

is a car advert. They must surely be minting it on these deals which are finance by another name?

Let's work it out the reality of affordability.

Firstly, on that average wage – that's what a typical person earns before tax - the after tax figure is probably only about £1,800 per month.

And if we round up the car figures a bit for ease of maths, let's say the period is 50 months and the deposit is £5,000. Well that deposit divided by 50 is equivalent really to being asked to pay another £100 per month, as you don't generally get the deposit back. So the car is **actually costing £350** a month or thereabouts.

And of course £350 as a proportion of £1800 income is **nearer to 20%** than the 10% initially expected.

I also think many people forget when buying things like luxurious cars that these should surely be financed out of surplus income **after you have paid all your bills** like rent or a mortgage, insurance, food, electricity, council tax, clothes. I think so anyway and on an income of say £1,800 how much might be left? Maybe £850 a month if you are lucky?

So all of a sudden that supposedly cheap affordable luxury car that on the telly seems like it's just 10% of your wages is now costing almost **50% of the surplus income** (£350 out of £800).

Let's forget the likelihood of most people having saved another £12,000 to buy the vehicle outright in 4 years' time (as that's another £250 a month) and assume that by then most people will probably want another new car more than they want to hand over wads of cash for the same old one, so we're all prey for the smooth car dealers.

The dealers often claim you'll probably build up spare equity if you want to hand back the old car and you can **use this as the deposit towards the next new car** – but as far as I can tell this is not guaranteed to build up any extra value and even if it does, it is very unlikely to equal the full deposit needed in four years' time, which by then could easily be £5-6000. So just to stay on the road you might suddenly have to find a lot of cash, either to pay out the £12,000 final payment or contribute towards a new deposit. Or you could just walk away and have lost the lot, but you'll have no car.

> NB. If you'd kept your own old car instead rather than being tempted by a new one on PCP / lease or hire purchase then even in four years' time, instead of handing it back and being worth nothing, it might still have a **residual value** of a couple of thousand pounds, and you'd still have a set of wheels!

So it seems to me to be far more sensible to keeping an old car, or buy a car outright using a cheap Bank loan, or look for a PCP car costing around **£150 a month.**

So instead of the Super Dooper XYZ Sportster it's a **Duster or an MG** most people should be getting, and they're not bad cars – I've even been looking at them myself for a future purchase a bit down the road, pun intended, when I'm done with my Aston and Alfa Romeo! I can afford something better but a car is needed for low cost reliable transport – and all brands offer that.

My own estimates suggest, that after taking into account things like the lost income you could earn on investing your cash versus buying a car with a bank loan or one of the latest PCP or leasing deals, then it typically **costs around 10% more overall than buying it yourself, plus if you buy**

it, it becomes your asset to control and you don't get sudden bills for damage!

If you are buying a car with cash or a loan it makes sense to **haggle** on the price – I managed to get **17.5% discount** off a new car, it turned out to be more than the dealer was actually making, so we had to re-negotiate with things like free mats, tax and petrol so they could at least make a small profit!

FACT 30. – *It's increasingly unusual, but cash will get you a discount*

Often you can get a Bank loan (or go somewhere like Zopa) to borrow at say 3% and then maybe get 5% off the cost of the new car for cash. That's **2% arbitrage** in your favour.

The dealers will of course often try and offload their own finance, often at a cheap cost, but you may be **losing out on any discount** opportunity on the price, or they'll play the old switcheroo and tie you into a deal with a high APR% and give you an over the top value for your old car. Just like buying mortgages or loans, the **only thing to think about really here is what is the TOTAL cost** you will be paying when you walk away from the car in a few years' time?

They will also try and foist things like Gap Insurance onto buyers – this covers the gap, if there is one, in the value an insurer will pay if your car is badly damaged versus how much may be outstanding to the finance company. They may charge as much as 10% of the value of the vehicle – and for what? IMHO its better to argue with the insurer about the pay-out in the rare event that you need to claim, so that's a low risk of happening, plus anyway Gap Insurance is irrelevant for most new or older cars – MoneySavingExpert explains why in more detail.

I have studied depreciation and our monthly costs of ownership for cars when writing this book and think my conclusions in general can be summed up as follows:

- Finance is the most expensive route.
- Buying new cars is next most expensive, if you change them frequently.
- Buying new and keeping the car for a decade works out about the same as buying older cars and changing them every few years – so it's tempting to change but perhaps better the devil you know?
- So keeping a car for a long time is generally a bit cheaper overall

Having an expensive and cheap car for different types of journeys doesn't actually make economic sense or for an easy life. It often works out at the same overall cost as just owning one expensive car (this assumes the expensive car is less fuel efficient) as you spend more on an expensive car in other ways and with just one car you save on doubling up on tax, insurance, servicing, MOTs for example. So if you don't do many miles, just have the expensive car; if you do a lot, stick to a cheaper car, not two! I've tried it and worked out the maths!

Other ways to save money

All of the following areas of expenditure can be quite significant so it's worth exploring ways to get the best bang for your buck right at the outset as it's not always easy to quantify afterwards if you've had value for money or a good deal.

FACT 31. – *Even the small stuff adds up – but not Soap!*

Telephony

FACT 32. – *Phones are a bit like Car Finance Plans*

It's hard to save money on your home phone as most of the operators seem to have onerous small print to stop you from switching and of course it's nigh on impossible to work out the true cost before you commit. Headline prices quoted are for the core service and they often lose little matters like monthly service charges and the costs for things like phone calls (remember those?) so far in the small print you can never find it. It's all about the monthly internet price – but that's often only half the monthly bill.

The message: tread carefully, try and read the small print beforehand; clarify anything you are unsure of by email (so you have proof later) and remember to sort out any problems within the **cooling off period**, (typically this is 28 days).

Ditto really with utilities – we were promised £300 bonus to switch to British Gas. Did it ever materialise?, of course not. So we are now with Co-Op Energy.

OK, back to phones, What about mobiles?

Because of companies like GiffGaff which have minimal small print and don't lock you into a contract at all, you can quit at a moment's notice, the big guys seem to be offering better and better contracts all the time, but it still makes sense to check the small print and see how long you have to pay for.

If you are getting a posh Apple handset or tablet, or the latest Samsung that retails at £800 but you can get it for only £10.00 deposit and £29.95 a month (for 24 months) remember, just like a car PCP car deal, this isn't really an almost free phone. On top of the £29.99 you will normally have a tariff package, say £15.00 a month for calls and data and maybe £5.00 a month insurance?

So over 2 years you will pay a minimum of £10 + £30*24 + £15*24 +£5*24 = £1,210 in total. Plus extras for things like premium rate numbers, directory enquiries. In effect then you'll have paid the full £800 for the handset and £17 a month to use it. You could instead probably get the handset for £750 somewhere and buy your usage from Tesco or GiffGaff for £10 a month, and with insurance on top you might be saving **10% on your mobile phone bills.** That may not seem a lot, but over a lifetime could be as much as:

> **£4,000 saved at today's prices**, just by not using bundled offers for convenience.

In our house we make good use of old handsets and hand me downs (and we tend not to download the latest software updates which quickly bloat handsets and stop them working) so until recently we were still successfully using a first generation iPhone when we could be on generation 10! I'd only get a 10, more correctly known as the iPhone X **if the company were paying**.

We also buy handsets direct from China via BangGood.com so Mrs H (while she is waiting for my business iPhone 7 to free up) is the not-so-proud owner of a Umi Super – similar to the iPhone in looks, but Android and about 90% cheaper. It's not as good, of course, and it only cost about £90, but does what's needed and that's £1000 saved. If we repeat that trick over a lifetime that might add up to maybe:

> **£20,000 saved** if you get a new phone every couple of years.

Plus of course there's no need for insurance on a lower cost phone when you can get a new one so inexpensively. And it looks great too.

Pensions

FACT 33. – *You can spend a lot on hidden charges*

I've talked a fair bit about pensions but honestly have not been able to conclude anything beyond everyone is after your money and you pay a lot for advice, and sometimes it doesn't even seem that good advice. Some of my pensions have done well with double digit annual returns, some badly, and there seems to be little rhyme nor reason as to which is which as they are all with supposedly good fund managers – as I have mentioned my overall return appears to be around 5.4%, so little different to the base rate – and if that's the average, think how badly some have done.

Relatives have a similar tale to tell so whilst I won't be avoiding pensions completely – we still invest small amounts in them each month – I have to be honest and say this is more because of the tax breaks and not wanting to leave any potential untapped (as I did with Save as You Earn and Profit Sharing schemes) than it is confidence that the financial services sector will look after my money.

The UK has amongst the poorest pensioners in the world (judged according to retirement Income as a proportion of the final working salary) and whilst our salaries are better than many countries, the disparities are not so great with some of our European neighbours at the top of the pensions league table. So what are places like Italy, Norway and Turkey doing that we are not? Isn't the UK supposedly a world leader in financial acumen? If so, why isn't it washing through to our pensioners?

I've concluded, probably wrongly, that a lot of wealth is being created in the sector but it's not ending up in the hands of the customers. So if it's not the pensioners or young savers benefiting it must surely be the government or the banks and over paid fund managers claiming their 1% or whatever?

Needless to say you can probably guess what kind of proportion of our retirement will be dependent upon **Ourselves versus the *Professionals*…..roughly 80 / 20% in our favour,** so I'll say no more!

> Lifetime Savings – A conservative **£80,000 if you go DIY?**
>
> NB. **This is NOT investment advice, just an estimate of what you might pay others.**

Health

If your employer has a health scheme or a so called Cash-Plan (which gives you benefits back when you visit the dentist, optician, physio and the like) then these are worth considering as a way of saving money. Obviously it's more expensive than relying on free from the NHS and you do get taxed on the benefit, but it's a useful perk if you remember to claim, which isn't difficult.

We receive circa £1,500 per annum of health cover and pay tax of about £50 a month – so it's worthwhile for us but an expensive mistake if you don't claim as you'll be taxed just for belonging!

Chapter 17

Day to Day Purchases

Day to day purchases may be more mundane but as the supermarkets never tire of telling us, it's easy to work out everyday savings and boy can these add up over time.

Lots of money saving websites exist so I wont dwell on repeating old advice again here, rather, as I have a reputation for being careful (mostly by my wife and daughter), I will list out a few of the little gems in our household and give an **estimate of how much they might add up to over a 40 year saving regime**, at today's prices – that is, the **real sum saved will be more**.

Grocery

I encourage Mrs H wherever possible to stock up on 3-for-2 offers, but only of things we like. I think we should and could make space for 6 of everything, irrespective of whether it's Branston Pickle or shampoo, she normally puts her foot down at 3 items!

If we assume at any one time 5% of your grocery or household shop could be on offer that might be around 2% of your budget saved, week in week out – provided you stick to things you need and will use up.

> Lifetime Savings **£5,000** – and I bet it's a lot more than that.

Plus you can save more if you pay by card, more on that later. Rola Cola / Own Brand

With me footing the bill my daughter lives on Coke, Dr Pepper, Sprite and Schweppes soft drinks whereas I will have an upper price in my mind, and won't ever go beyond it. So as an example I won't on principle spend more than £1 on a 2 litre bottle of drink or 6 cans, and if it's more expensive I will switch brands or change to another drink until I find one on offer, or I will go without. We would rarely go Rola (if that is indeed a real brand anymore?) or own brand as there is no point buying something you don't like but I can see no harm in switching what you like in alignment with Offers?

And let's face it, with so much choice in the shops there is always something nice on offer or a perfectly acceptable alternative that tastes almost the same if you were blindfolded?

I have noticed too that I can buy brands like Carters Lemonade, famous years ago, but less so now, so better than own brand but not as nice as Schweppes – for just £0.20, so why wouldn't you?

> Lifetime Savings **£3,000** – and that's without sinking as low as we could!

Petrol prices

There is simply no point driving around to save money on fuel as the extra mileage travelled will usually use up more than the money you save by shopping around, say 2p per litre. But if you take the **opportunity to fill up when you pass a lower cost garage**, it adds up, and that's even if you are not obsessive about noting the price everywhere all the time – it's enough to just have a feel for which are the slightly better value garages in your area or on your route to work.

> Lifetime savings **£2,000** on an average mileage.

I have looked at Fuel Cards as a way of helping employees save money, but it doesn't seem to stack up that well.

Buying fuel and other things like Groceries on a **Cash Back card**, makes great sense. I use American Express in big business and Barclaycard Visa in smaller outlets, and these earn me **1% and 0.5% cashback** respectively – but it adds up to about £200 a year, almost enough for a weekend break.

> NB. It's important to remember to pay off the card each month – we do this by Direct Debit hence never pay interest to anyone, they pay us free money.

You can also achieve something similar with a **Pre-Paid** Visa or MasterCard (where you load money on in advance and then spend it) available via companies like TelecomPlus, my old client. Here it's impossible to go into debt or forget to pay.

> Lifetime savings / earnings circa **£8,000** just by choosing cards.

> PS. It is also true that I do **coast my car down long hills** (but leave the engine on so things like power steering, brakes and safety systems still work). I've been told by a techy friend it's pointless as the engine can tell when it doesn't need fuel so stops pumping it anyway, but I'm not so sure and on occasions have been able to freewheel for a mile. If cars do 30 to the gallon and its £6.00 a gallon then that's £0.20 saved each time.

> Lifetime savings **£8,000**, but not recommended!

Entertainment

Do you really need all those channels and services on your TV? And what about HD, can you tell the difference in picture quality on most programs? If you're not sure it's easy to shave maybe £20 a month of these costs.

Lifetime Savings a surprising **£10,000**

If you like popping out for a cake and a coffee or a meal out, I know people who will intentionally pick the most expensive thing off the menu (seemingly mostly just to prove they can afford it to themselves) even if they actually prefer to eat something else. Why not stop doing that and if something is on offer, even if it's your second favourite, go for that instead? Whatever you consume is generally forgotten within hours, the people you mix with matter more.

Lifetime Savings – at say 30%, maybe as much as **£18,000** saved

Ditto why not go to the 2-4-£10 or similar restaurant if you like their food better than the nearby posh restaurant? The ingredients often come from the exact same wholesalers – it's just served in a nicer atmosphere with quieter clientele!

Lifetime Savings - **£10,000**

Newspapers

Everyone used to buy these every day, it's less common now and we down-graded years ago, firstly to just weekend papers, then Sundays only. Now we have nothing. Even if you go from having a daily paper to just a weekend one, you won't miss it much and the savings add up.

Lifetime savings **£6,000**

Drinking

A couple of drinks in the pub, coffee shop or a bottle of wine at home can easily exceed £6 a day. Even if you could just halve that habit it would have a huge impact and be great for your health too.

We still like to have a coffee over a good book but plenty of **sachet drinks** can be bought from the likes of Nescafe, Kenco or even at Aldi and Lidl and the bigger supermarkets, for around £0.10-£0.15 per drink. It's a lot cheaper than going out or using a pod system and again, it adds up to a lot more than you'd think. Imagine if this money was invested instead – it could buy a house!

>Lifetime Savings **£45,000**

Council Tax & Regulatory Stuff

Some of these charges are based on weird historical facts, so for example your property's Council Tax is based on the perceived value of the property in **1991,** even if it wasn't built then. We appealed our valuation on the strength of an arithmetic anomaly in the Council's figures and accordingly pay less tax each year than neighbours whose houses sold for less when they were built.

> Lifetime savings **£17,000** – and it might impact water rates too.

Another way of saving money on what I term regulatory stuff is employing an accountant as soon as you possibly can, and even if it's only for your personal tax returns. They are aware of all the little tricks used by the authorities to catch you out with complex wording plus of course can help you maximise any advantages if you start up or run a business, even if it's just a dabble in Multi-Level Marketing or Party Plan from home.

You can legally offset some of your household living costs (not food but things like council tax, energy bills, computer costs) dependent upon how much space this part time business occupies at home – I think we claim for part of one room, this being a study.

You'll be surprised at how the savings add up. Plus of course at Tax Return time we avoid all that hassle and uncertainty of doing it ourselves, provided of course you use a reputable professional, not a dodgy tax avoider.

Simple tax affairs are typically managed for about £500 for a couple, £1,000 if you add on a simple business.

Lifetime Savings – might be as much as **£20,000**

Toiletries

Yes its true I decant my cheaper (Aldi) shampoo and bubble bath into more expensive bottles such as Radox.

And I have a toothpaste squeezer (£1 on eBay): https://www.ebay.co.uk/i/361715432932?chn=ps to extract the last drops...

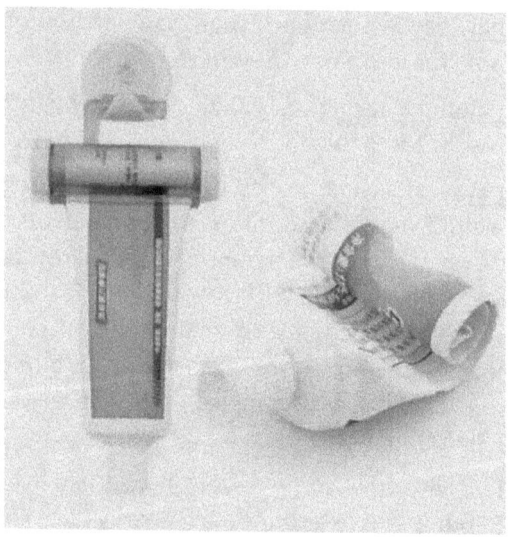

.... and a soap press for making use of those left over fiddly bits (sadly only available at Amazon).

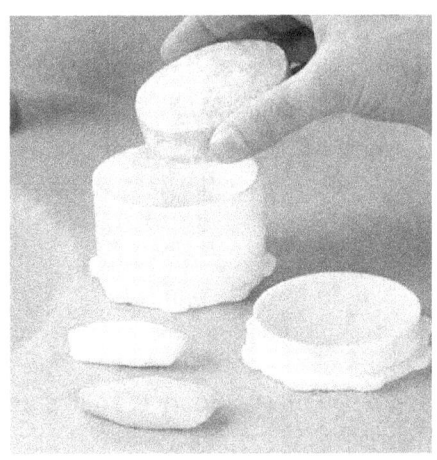

https://www.amazon.co.uk/Soap-Saver-Bar-Mould-Recycle/dp/B00N9XRWWY)

but contrary to public opinion I do all these things not to save money but because I like being **eco-friendly** and enjoy the nicer bottles. That's my story anyway.

> Lifetime savings a whopping **£100,** Lifetime enjoyment, **Priceless**

Clothes

We buy from a mix of upmarket brands and the likes of Primark and it's sometimes hard to tell the difference. And we prefer shopping in an outlet village, like Bicester near Oxford, than in the designer shops themselves as these seem to be full of snooty sales assistants and snootier customers.

> Lifetime Savings – circa **£15,000** for 3 of us, as we don't shop much

Warranties

I've always being a big believer in having insurance for everything, including product breakdowns, as I hate being surprised with bills and would rather pay through the nose to avoid nasty surprises at the least opportune moment.

Over the years we have used various companies, British Gas, Domestic and General, warranty Direct, 247 Home Rescue. Other than the last company I would consider most of these firms do offer a genuinely good service, albeit the inevitable small print seems to be getting more prevalent. In the cold light of day I don't believe we have saved any money here, just peace of mind. I won't comment on the last company as I am about to take them to the Small Claims Court for misrepresenting what they sell.

I've recently benchmarked the costs of claims if I had gone to a repair company direct, and including call out charges it worked out at about £85 a job versus the £75 excess charged by companies like 247, plus a £700 per annum contract. Plainly it is cheaper to pay yourself.

> Lifetime Savings – **£5,000** (If you forget warranties and save the money instead)

Re other insurances, I have concluded extended **Car Warranties** are in fact a huge waste of time, money and effort as they put so many hurdles in your way to make a claim and then generally deduct big excesses, you may just as well save the money yourself into an investment account, hope you get to save long enough before you need it, and cash in the emergency fund profits after – or use it towards a new purchase. Plus you'll earn interest on your money too.

> Lifetime savings – **£15,000** if you avoid car warranties, other than free ones on new cars!

With products like **Life Insurance**, it's worth shopping around online and also don't rule out talking to a real broker – they know the secrets of the trade and can drive out a good deal, especially if your circumstances are a little unusual.

>Lifetime savings **£5,000** for two.

Utilities

With energy being a global business and whoever pays the most getting the energy, it's hardly surprising that all our bills keep on rising. I think what the switching services tell us is absolutely true: you will benefit from **regular** switching, albeit it's a bit of a hassle. Conversely by not switching I think we are exposed to hidden price hikes in just the same way (but in reverse) that the Banks and Building Societies lower their interest rates when we are not looking. If you stay put, you will get fleeced.

I **don't believe** the comparison sites always show the best deals, as they presumably make different commission amounts from each supplier, so it's worth checking the lists carefully, looking at the small print, and switching every couple of years.

> Lifetime Savings **£8,000** but will vary on property and household size.

I'm not convinced Smart Meters will make any difference to consumption!

Books

We buy a lot of books but unlike my daughter who loves the smell of shops like Waterstones (and pays for the privilege) we tend to buy from the special offer section at the local supermarket or Smiths newsagents, or better still from BookPeople where it's not uncommon to only pay £2.00 for a new paperback.

On average we probably read one book a week each so we probably generally save £4.00 on each. I have also been known to add to my PG Wodehouse collection on eBay but you won't catch Mrs H reading second hand or old library books!

>Lifetime Savings **£8,000**

Total Savings?

FACT 34. – *Enough to buy a House?*

If my mathematics are right, ignoring money wasted on warranties, than that little lot adds up to about **£290,000 over a 40 year period, so that's £7,000 per annum** and not far off £125 a week saved. It's not a huge amount but is the basis on which a wealthier future can easily be based, and you'd hardly notice you were saving.

If I remember correctly we started out by saving about £100 a month on our journey with you here and then gradually increased it to around double that by putting money into pensions, savings and investments of various kinds?

So it just goes to show, taking a sensible approach to everyday purchases without dramatically altering your life can all add up. And if you skimp on things like we have done, such as entertainment, holidays, expensive jewellery, it can all come together as a plan even quicker.

Adding in savings by looking for cheaper mortgage lenders or better car deals becomes further icing on the cake towards anyone becoming a millionaire, even on an Average Wage.

Chapter 18
Keeping Stuff a Long Time

Whilst its tempting to always want the latest iPad or follow the latest fashion in home décor we tend to only buy things when it becomes **necessary**, and in the case of something that is broken or worn out, we will generally try and **repair** it first before replacing.

I have analysed our 100 most visible / memorable purchases, excluding clothing, jewellery and holidays, so this is what I would call **STUFF**, you know, the things you need to live but that aren't necessities like heating, light, food, council tax, or indeed the house itself.

So our top 100 does include things like car purchases, buying a new hi-fi or fridge freezer, replacing furniture or curtains because they are worn out or we fancy a change or recent things like say a kettle breaking or adding a conservatory. So it's a mix of large and small and you'd be surprised at what a large proportion of your assets can be totted up in just **100 items**, I reckon close to **75%** (plus clothes for example) so you don't need to tot up everything.

What I discovered is that even including things like cars and kitting out a kitchen with appliances and a lounge, dining room or bedroom with furniture, on average:

> **We don't spend more than 10% of our income per year on stuff.**

The average amount per item is **£1,100 (or £620 if we exclude cars)** and we only make such a purchase (always with cash/cards, never on credit) **every 21 weeks**, so only about **2.5 times per year**.

And we **stick with our purchases**.

On average we keep things for just over 10 years.

Even cheaper items (say under £100) don't get thrown away until they've given around 7 years' service whereas more expensive items (average £1,650) are expected to last **17 years,** or about £100 per year. I don't think we could be described as profligate in the slightest?

> **Editor's note** – that's interesting, have you noticed that on the bigger items you've hit that magic £100 number again so not so different to your monthly target car depreciation rate, target savings rate or your planned daily holiday cost! Have you got a thing for the number 100?
>
> **Author's note** – I didn't think so until you pointed it out, maybe that's why I like percentages and cumulative growth so much?.....And digital marketing is of course similar to decimals, it's all 1's and 0's apparently!

My final word on this topic: it transpires, which I didn't realise before doing the research for you, is that as a **Rule of Thumb I don't expect any of our assets / possessions to cost us more than £0.20-£0.50** per day, any more than that and it has to be an accumulating asset that grows in value like a property extension – my cars of course being the exception!

So as an example, I could of course these days afford a £4,000 watch but at that price it would have to last between 8,000 and 20,000 days....so that's **22-60 years**, neither of which seems likely. So my favourite watch cost me about £225 and as if by magic that equals 450-1,200 days. I've had it 4 years, so that's spot on!

Chapter 19
Refunds

Some years ago I worked with a lovely lady in a large London advertising agency, she earned big bucks, so did her husband in the City. She was always impeccably turned out and seemed to have dozens of different outfits of clothes. The truth was she had thousands of mostly unworn garments at home. She was time poor, cash rich, plus she had a touch of OCD or similar, so when she spotted something in a shop she liked she would snap up several colours and several sizes, plus anything matching, in the hope that something fitted.

But she never took anything back, so she had clothes in the surrounding sizes that were unworn and sometimes even the whole set if nothing fitted. She literally had thousands of unworn items taking up space and wasting money.

Now I don't know if her story had a happy ending and she got over her spending habits or OCD problems, or they ran out of money or space. It doesn't matter but on a smaller scale many people are like this: they won't take faulty products back, exchange things or complain over small amounts. The reason I bring this matter up is that even small amounts, due to the power of compound interest, can form the basis of a nest egg or add up as a huge waste, like a loan.

Selling old things on eBay isn't for everyone – I only use it for books and DVDs – and for me it's more about freeing up space and earning more cash for charity donations than giving items instead to the doorstep jumble collectors who I'm sure rip everyone off – the point is every little helps.

In our household I have a few famous or infamous examples which my daughter loves to tell people about – so I may as well share them here too.

The Faux Sheep

I once bought sheepskin seat covers for my Mini from a local car accessory shop, fitted them, then saw them 30% cheaper at Argos. So I bought an identical set at Argos and took the Argos ones back to the accessory shop for a refund as if they were the first set.

Kerching, at today's prices that's £10 saved!

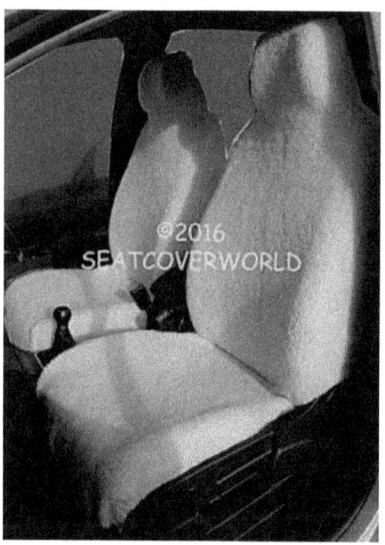

The Dead Tree

Its true, we bought a huge tree from the local garden centre and took it back after a couple of weeks when it started to drop and die. Obviously we transported it poking through the sun-roof of an expensive car, as you do.

Refund £50.00

Editor's note – How else would you do it?

Wilting Tree!

The Album

Its also true that I did once take an album back to the record shop and was allegedly overheard saying, "This is c**p, can I change it for something else?" The bewildered sales assistant was obviously too shocked to say No!

The Jam, obviously!

The Dead Budgie

Yes, you read that right. We bought a lovely budgie from a pet shop, called him Billy Wiz, except he didn't wiz, he just sat on my finger and died. Imagine the surprise at the

Customer Service department to be presented with a small box, only to open it and see poor old Billy with a glassy stare looking up at them. Refund £45, or we might have had a replacement budgie – I can't recall – but we certainly didn't name the next one Wiz, just in case.

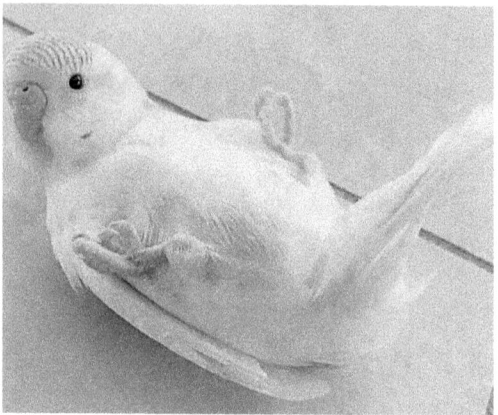

This isn't Billy!

It turned out that pet shops buy up aviaries of birds and sell them onto the unsuspecting public as if they were new freshly minted budgies, so ours was probably a pensioner when we got him!

Chapter 20

Where has the wealth ended up?

This is not a perfect science (as I haven't recorded every single penny spent on a packet of polos for example) and it's a fact that we haven't spent inheritances on cars (but perhaps having extra cash in gave us the confidence to spend our own savings in a more frivolous manner) but the following represents a visual explanation of money in and out.

The arrows denote where most of said income flowed, so as an example wages went into property purchase, savings (via contributory and non-contributory pensions) and investments.

The investments in turn grew which enabled us to invest in business, and the businesses grew enabling us to make investments in property from which we receive a retirement income in the form of rent, after costs are deducted of course. I have tried to make each box size represent the size of fund and highlighted in grey those with the best annual returns in our experience.

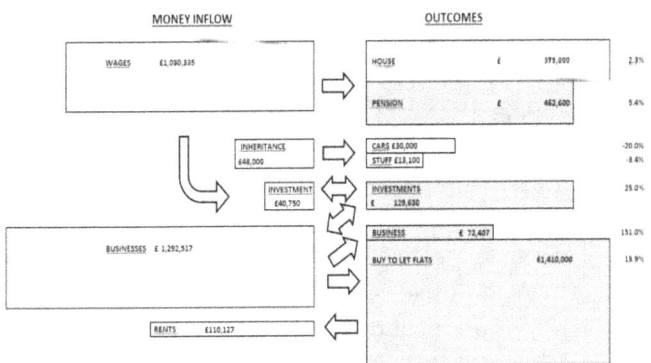

The Annual Rates of Return are on the right hand side.

As you can hopefully digest, wages went on the family home and pension.

Stuff, as alluded to previously, including cars, loses money so is generally not an appreciating asset.

FACT 35. – *Money does indeed make money*

If we had not started to save from an early date we would not have been able to invest the circa £80,000 growth from said investments into business.

So whilst technically we would still, as a family, be classed as millionaires (from the combined value of the family home and pensions) we would indeed have still achieved the somewhat odd distinction, as mentioned in the Introduction, of creating wealth circa **11% more than we have ever jointly earned, even if we'd not spent a penny.**

But by saving and investing more we eventually added £1.2m extra profit from businesses which has in turn created £300,000 growth in subsequently acquired properties and circa £100,000 additional income for retirement, this being the net rental income earned after taxes, agents fees, void periods, repairs, service charges and so on.

> NB. I estimate investment property only delivers **around 50% of the rent as income**, less so of course after mortgages and insurance have been paid, so whilst generally I regard it as a great investment, it is not quite as lucrative as people imagine and hence only worth taking small risks with. To me it seems a great place for savings, but I wouldn't over commit ourselves in the hope of profits as prices can fall and tenants do sometimes fail to pay (circa 2% of the time in our case)

Our property assets should of course continue to grow in value over time and earn more revenue, so I believe it's still attractive as an investment category and should remain so until we start building enough new property for everyone in the UK.

In short, saving small amounts of money has turned millionaires into multi- millionaires. Our total asset value is today worth circa **260% times more than we've ever earned** and a whopping 15,000% more than the £18,000 surplus that never was at the start of this book documenting our journey through our finances.

Chapter 21

Would I do it like this again?

Not exactly.

We know that compared to most people we know we have lived too frugal a life with few holidays, not many brand new cars or treats. Whilst in part this has been created by family health circumstances, we certainly could and should have pushed the boat out in more ways more often – and as I have said already, you can't take it with you so to a degree it certainly makes sense to make your money deliver happiness for yourself or others rather than save it like a miser.

That said, I am also a firm believer in planning for the future and being financially independent rather than relying on others help at some unspecified date in the future – be that family, friends or even the government with pensions and adult care.

In my mid-thirties I set a goal to be **financially free and independent by the age of 50,** so that means I wanted to have the freedom at that age to jack in my job if I so chose and retire on a modest income. It didn't mean I would, but I wanted **choices**.

I didn't achieve that goal exactly but by a mixture of good planning, good networking, and some good fortune I was able to achieve this goal at the age of **51 years**. So whilst some fun has been missed over the years I can at least take comfort now that I only need to go into work because I want to and **like working** with my colleagues, clients and contacts.

That is a huge stress reliever and looking back I have realised some of the most chilled people I have ever worked with were the ones who, whilst we had no idea at the time, actually didn't need to be there – generally being from wealthy families or having had large inheritances or a win on the lottery.

> **Editor's note** – well remembered, Lottery, is that part of your financial plan?
>
> **Author's note** – Actually it's not. I believe in taking control of finances and the lottery is trusting to luck. A modest win won't impact our circumstances beyond getting a newer nice car so I don't partake in paying the government yet more tax. We do encourage our daughter to take part though – she has had so much bad luck that a £1m win would change her life completely as she is young.

Back to the plot.

So I think planning is important and whilst I would do some things differently I think overall I would still have been a saver.

FACT 36. – *Saving is not a diet.*

This is because saving isn't like a diet whereby you are giving up on something, with saving, if it is done well, you get to enjoy whatever you didn't enjoy now, but at a later date, and then you might get to keep on enjoying repeats forever.

> **Author's note** – not the best analogy ever, diets and repeating!

What I mean is once an investment starts to grow you can withdraw from it regularly and keep on buying more or the thing you gave up one of at the beginning, or something else of course!

So in my mind Saving is in fact akin to being on the kind of diet that rewards you with many more cakes down the road!

By being a saver you might also benefit from lower costs and an ability to negotiate harder at a later date as products generally get **cheaper** over time and as I have said already, cash is king when it comes to **negotiating** a price cut. And that saved money means you get to buy something else at a later date too.

The other benefit of saving is that whilst initially, yes, you do consume less, you get to **plan what you might buy** at a later date when you have the cash, only to find that you might not actually go ahead so you get to plan again, effectively spending the **same money many times**. I find savouring the moment multiple times is in fact more enjoyable than the single gratification you get from an immediate once only purchase..

Assuming amassing some wealth remained a goal then, how might I have varied my strategy at the start if I had known now the facts that I think this book's research has taught me and our dear readers?

- One thing I would alter is moving up market and **changing the family home** – I feel we did this too often and in fact **moved once to many times** so we now need to consider downsizing in older age. If we'd stayed put in an earlier cheaper house, we could have still had a very nice home in a good area, but would have benefited from less maintenance and running costs, and the money saved (on this) plus money not spent on investing further equity plus an increased mortgage could have been **redirected** instead, years earlier, into the Buy To Let property market.

I estimate if we had done this at various opportune times we might have achieved circa **20%-300% more wealth overall** and would own between 3 and 50 more properties achieving up to a 300% larger retirement income – so that's a lot of extra wealth to potentially bequeath to family or a charitable trust. So we've been a bit selfish there by spending instead on our home now! The vast range of these numbers is indicative of how much property prices have risen in 40 years and even if we'd picked up on this fact late on, an extra 20% in retirement isn't to be sniffed at!

- Another thing I would have done differently is place less trust in financial advisors and more trust in my own ability to manage investments or at the very least track down high interest earning accounts.

I don't know if its because of all the charges levied or because I've just been unlucky but these professionals seem to have made pretty woeful returns on investment and I could hardly have done much worse using a pin.

- A third thing we would have done relates to business. Some of the income not spent on our own home or pensions would have been put earlier into businesses.
- It doesn't matter if I hadn't got an idea for a business myself, we all know a mate down the pub who is about to branch out as his own boss as a plumber or a mechanic or a web designer and it's a relatively simple matter to lend somebody a few hundred or thousand pounds in return for a stake in their business. Most of these investments will barely pay back the loan, some will go bust, friends will cease to be friends, but one or two ideas become the next Pimlico Plumbers, Reggae

Reggae Sauce or Amazon. Or in my old boss's case, Asda.
- Even a modest business success can make you millions for the simple reason that businesses tend to be acquired for multiples of their profit or turnover on the assumption that a new owner can milk it for X years.

So as an example, you might own 10% of a business turning over £100,000 a month, £1.2m a year. But it might sell for 500% of that turnover figure (its also common to use a multiple of profit – I think our main business fetched 15 X multiple when sold) so the business might sell, say, to a competitor, for £6m and your 10% is suddenly worth £600,000 or over half a million after tax. That would take a lot of saving but might have only cost a punt of £1,000 on a friend. And you might have had the £1,000 back years earlier too.

> **Wealth Warning**. Investing in businesses is very risky – Roughly 20% of new business fail in Year 1 and **only 50% survive for 5 Years**. To me this suggests it's unwise to put all your eggs in one basket, however much a sure thing it is (reread the section on Hot Tips if you need reminding!) and you certainly shouldn't invest too much or too big a proportion of your total savings into businesses. But it's worth a punt to make you wealthy.

Even the paperwork for a simple Agreement isn't as daunting as it once was – lots of free templates can be found online or I use a Notary Public (sort of like a high end lawyer but they often charge less than a law firm as they can work from home) who tidies up what I write down in a simple letter. It is worth having an Agreement and even considering setting up a Limited Company for all your ventures (remember those tax advantages) as it's easy and low cost, plus it helps ring-fence your private assets from those of your business associates (who may have hidden personal debts) that could bite you if it were a partnership or undocumented agreement. I've seen people lose the family home by ignoring this kind of risk and seeing a fraudulent partner escape scot free with their money whilst they carry the can.

In summary, if I was doing all this again and with hindsight, I would probably **aim for the following** levels of expenditure versus saving:

TABLE 13.

	We Spent	HindSight Spending	Change
Home	44%	28%	-16%
Food/ Clothes/ Health	15%	15%	0%
Transport	14%	15%	1%
Savings /Investment /Pensions	13%	10%	-3%
Leisure/Fun/Phones	5%	6%	1%
Businesses	2%	6%	4%
Presents	3%	3%	0%
Tax Contingency Savings	3%	3%	0%
Rental Properties	0%	12%	12%
Charity	2%	2%	0%
	100%	100%	
Savings Total	18%	31%	

As you can see, I would propose to commit **16% less expenditure on our own home**, most of which is diverted into acquiring property to rent out, 3% less in savings (by this I mean managed savings via other people and pension funds) to be replaced by a **4% increase in investments in my own or others' business ventures**, possibly via an online crowdfunding marketplace such as **Seedrs.com** if I couldn't identify opportunities myself.

So whilst I stated a minute ago I would have done some things differently with more fun, actually If I had my time again with this knowledge, I would **increase the amount of cash we saved from 18% of expenditure to 31%,** (so that looks like less fun surely?) but we'd still have a **bit more fun** by increasing our spending (by staying put in a smaller house) on things like **phones and cars and holidays**.

If you've got this far Victoria and Ali, an easy point to remember is every time you think of spending some money on a gadget, save the same amount on one side to invest in a business somewhere!

And for every £ you spend on things like **food and clothing**, try and save a similar amount in an investment account to put towards your first property or once you have that, buy to let properties.

Anything else that's left after at, its fine to squander on frivolous things!

Simple.

If that's how someone on average wages can become a multi-millionaire it should surely be a simple matter for brainier people or those on above average wages already to get be an millionaire, and maybe beyond too?

Chapter 22

Risk

I couldn't finish the book without saying a few words about risk. If my daughter, friend or anyone else reading this far (thanks by the way, firstly for buying the book and secondly for persevering this far) goes on to became a saver and investor then I think its important to incorporate the following into your money management philosophy too:

- Assume **everyone is after your hard earned money** – whether its an advisor (on commission, hidden or declared), someone recommending a hot-tip (as they probably already own assets in the business) or a potential business partner who doesn't tell you all the pitfalls – they can all cost you dear.
- Assume things will go wrong – so minimise this by **not cutting corners** on your research, due diligence or paperwork, and don't take anything at face value – whether it's a product or a person. Ask difficult questions, get things in writing or email as a back-up.
- **Don't put all your eggs in one basket**. As you can tell from the hundreds of different types of investment we have owned over the decades I feel it is important not to bet everything on one thing – if that went wrong you don't want to be faced with starting again late in life. So don't put all your eggs into property, or buy to let, or pensions, or businesses. Try and do a bit of everything.
- Don't be afraid of doing more yourself. Financial matters are complicated but we're not putting a man on the moon here. Cut risk by always considering the **Total Costs**.

- Remember savings isn't a punishment or a diet – you are merely taking breadth before spending even more in future, assuming you've got the money of course.

But don't let all this caution put you off. Saving and investing can be fun and it's a great feeling having enough cash in the Bank so that it doesn't matter if your next salary is paid a week late or the fridge needs fixing, and even better to ponder things you might buy, but then persuade yourself not to, only to get to do it again by theoretically spending the money again!

Footnote

I know I promised to give up my version of day trading but its harder than I thought when in just a few days I made the equivalent to 27% pa return, for just a few minutes work!

In the last days of the book I bought two shares (SSE and Vodafone), kept them a week and have sold them today for a modest £16 and £12 profit respectively. Not a lot of profit but if I scaled up the time spent it works out at about an equivalent salary to being on **£175,000 per annum**. Plus I didn't risk much and I can now afford to take Mrs H for another coffee and maybe even throw in a bit of carrot cake!

Summary

The Average Wage Millionaire

Can *anyone* really get rich?

Let's summarise briefly what I hope the book has hopefully explained adequately in detail – but please remember this is not financial advice!

- It would indeed appear that it is **entirely possible** to set out to become a millionaire even if you only earn an average wage, enjoy no special luck and get no large hand-outs or business successes. If you get those too, you're surely sorted!
- We've seen it's vital though to become a **regular saver**, or to put it another way, to become a **delayed spender** and whilst you don't need to become a penny pincher, you do need to become aware of value as **every penny saved counts**.
- It's important to **buy from your own money** than to use credit and much better to **earn interest** than pay it, unless it's for an appreciating asset that goes up in value – otherwise you are just making somebody else rich at your expense.
- The discipline of saving isn't a punishment like dieting, it actually increases your opportunities for enjoyment, it's like a **Secret Club to consume more**.
- If you can save, or shall we say redirect, **20% of your income**, you can potentially create **wealth** for yourself, your family or good causes but also **reduce stress** and fears of things like redundancy or illness at work.
- If you can master the techniques of **smarter buying**, **changing** things around regularly (but **not buying new stuff too often**) then it's possible to accumulate wealth

beyond all your total earnings and grasping the power of cumulative mathematics will change your life as it's the difference between **rich and poor**.

- Spending a few **minutes really can save you years**, and also remember to check out the **total costs** of ownership and consider the likely **cost per day** or everything you do.

Finally we've learnt to beware hot tips, trust yourself more but don't put all your eggs into one basket!

That's it, I think you're good to go!

Art Rain

Appendices of useful links

https://www.ageuk.org.uk/information-advice/money-legal/pensions/changes-to-state-pension-age/

https://www.weforum.org/agenda/2015/11/what-is-the-future-of-money/ 26 Nov 2015 - Our perception of MONEY – how it is earned and ITS VALUE – is undergoing a major ... more than 600 in the last 30 years, and the TREND continues.

inflation.iamkate.com/ View the HISTORY of UK INFLATION RATES and convert prices between any year in the range 1751 to 2018.

https://www.valuepenguin.com/loans/difference-between-apr-and-interest-rate Most credit cards have average APRs between 12% AND 25% AND have a monthly billing cycle. However, INTEREST on credit card debt is charged only on the ...

https://www.theguardian.com/cities/2018/jul/04/is-bezos-holding-seattle-hostage-the-cost-of-being-amazons-home

https://www.moneyexpert.com/savings-accounts/national-savings-and-investment-nsi/
National Savings and Investment (NS&I) *National savings* and investment is a government backed form of *savings* account, meaning that they offer a secure way to store your money away. They benefit from having no limit to the amount that the government will protect, in contrast to normal bank's *savings* accounts.

https://www.thesun.co.uk/archives/news/729849/the-word-of-hod/

BBC News - Have prime ministers ever been well paid? news.bbc.co.uk/2/hi/uk_news/magazine/8715505.stm

https://www.npr.org/sections/krulwich/2012/09/15/160879929/that-old-rice-grains-on-the-chessboard-con-with-a-new-twist?t=1530807986043

https://www.ft.com/content/34859346-b023-11e7-8076-0a4bdda92ca2 3 Mar 2006 - His train ticket to Oxford has dropped in price from MB 50 to MB 35 over the forty years. But a helping of roast beef and Yorkshire pudding at ...

https://www.moneysavingexpert.com/car-insurance/gap-insurance/

https://www.citizensadvice.org.uk/.../refund-time-limit-will-help-consumers-get-their-...
13 May 2014 - A set time limit on when *refunds* need to be paid, as recommended by Citizens Advice, will help people uphold their rights and *get money back* ...

https://www.seedrs.com/ Online investing opportunities in the best new start-up businesses, and raise seed and angel investment, with top European equity crowdfunding site Seedrs.com

https://vegasclick.com/gambling/martingale-betting-system The Martingale betting system increases your chances of winning in the short term. It's a fact. How can we say this when the most respected gambling math ...

https://www.fool.com/careers/.../what-percentage-of-businesses-fail-in-their-first.aspx 3 May 2017 - Perhaps the scariest thing of all is knowing that most businesses won't be successful. What's the percentage of businesses that fail in their first ...

Bite-Sized Business Books are designed to provide practical support and insights for professionals who are tackling an unfamiliar task either for the first time or after a gap, as well as those who want to find new ways of doing what they are familiar with. They are deliberately short, easy to read books guiding the reader through the various stages behind each business process or activity, with a clear focus on outcomes. They are firmly based on personal experience and success.

The most successful people all share an ability to focus on what really matters, keeping things simple and understandable. MBAs, metrics and methodologies have their place, but when we are faced with a new challenge most of us need quick guidance on what matters most, from people who have been there before and who can show us where to start. As Stephen Covey famously said, "The main thing is to keep the main thing, the main thing." But what exactly is the main thing?

Bite-Sized books were conceived to help answer precisely that question crisply and fast and, of course, be engaging to read, written by people who are experienced and successful in their field.

The brief? Distil the *main things* into a book that can be read by an intelligent non-expert comfortably in around 60 minutes. Make sure the book enables the reader with specific tools, ideas and plenty of examples drawn from real life and business. Be a virtual mentor.

Bite-Sized Books don't cover every eventuality, but they are written from the heart by successful people who are happy to share their experience with you and give you the benefit of their success.

We have avoided jargon – or explained it – and made few assumptions about the reader, except that they are in business, are literate and numerate, and that they can adapt and use what we suggest to suit their own, individual purposes. Whether you are working for a multi-national corporation or a start-up or something in between, the principles we introduce will hold good.

They can be read straight through at one easy sitting and then used as a support while you are working on what you need to do.

Bite-Sized Books Catalogue

Business Books

Ian Benn
>   Write to Win
>   > How to Produce Winning Proposals and RFP Responses

Matthew T Brown
>   Understand Your Organisation
>   > An Introduction to Enterprise Architecture Modelling

David Cotton
>   Rethinking Leadership
>   > Collaborative Leadership for Millennials and Beyond

Richard Cribb
>   IT Outsourcing: 11 Short Steps to Success
>   > An Insider's View

Phil Davies
>   How to Survive and Thrive as a Project Manager
>   > The Guide for Successful Project Managers

Paul Davies
>   Developing a Business Case
>   > Making a Persuasive Argument out of Your Numbers

Paul Davies
> Developing a Business Plan
>> Making a Persuasive Case for Your Business

Paul Davies
> Contract Management for Non-Specialists

Paul Davies
> Developing Personal Effectiveness in Business

Paul Davies
> A More Effective Sales Team
>> Sales Management Focused on Sales People

Tim Emmett
> Bid for Success
>> Building the Right Strategy and Team

Nigel Greenwood
> Why You Should Welcome Customer Complaints
>> And What to Do About Them

Nigel Greenwood
> Six Things that All Customer Want
>> A Practical Guide to Delivering Simply Brilliant Customer Service

Stuart Haining
> The Practical Digital Marketeer – Volume 1
>> Digital Marketing – Is It Worth It and Your First Steps

Stuart Haining
> The Practical Digital Marketeer – Volume 2
>> Planning for Success

Stuart Haining
> The Practical Digital Marketeer – Volume 3
>> Your Website

Stuart Haining
> The Practical Digital Marketeer – Volume 4
>> Be Sociable – Even If You Hate It

Stuart Haining
> The Practical Digital Marketeer – Volume 5
>> Your On-going Digital Marketing

Christopher Hosford
> Great Business Meetings! Greater Business Results
>> Transforming Boring Time-Wasters into Dynamic Productivity Engines

Ian Hucker
> Risk Management in IT Outsourcing
>> 9 Short Steps to Success

Marcus Lopes and Carlos Ponce
> Retail Wars
>> May the Mobile be with You

Maiqi Ma
> Win with China
>> Acclimatisation for Mutual Success Doing Business with China

Elena Mihajloska
> Bridging the Virtual Gap
>> Building Unity and Trust in Remote Teams

Rob Morley
> Agile in Business
>> A Guide for Company Leadership

Gillian Perry
> Managing the People Side of Change
>> Ten Short Steps to Success in IT Outsourcing

Art Rain
> The Average Wage Millionaire
>> Can *Ayone* Really Get Rich

Saibal Sen
> Next Generation Service Management
>> An Analytics Driven Approach

Don Sharp
> Nothing Happens Until You Sell Something
>> A Personal View of Selling Techniques

Christopher Hosford
> Great Business Meetings! Greater Business Results
>> Transforming Boring Time-Wasters into Dynamic Productivity Engines

Lifestyle Books

Anna Corthout
> Alive Again
>> My Journey to Recovery

Phil Davies
> Don't Worry Be Happy
>> A Personal Journey

Phil Davies
> Feel the Fear and Pack Anyway
>> Around the World in 284 Days

Regina Kerschbaumer
> Yoga Coffee and a Glass of Wine
>> A Yoga Journey

Gillian Perry
> Capturing the Celestial Lights
>> A Practical Guide to Imagining the Northern Lights

Arthur Worrell
> A Grandfather's Story
>> Arthur Worrell's War

Public Affairs Books

Eben Black
- Lies Lunch and Lobbying
  - PR, Public Affairs and Political Engagement – A Guide

John Mair and Richard Lance Keeble – Editors
- Investigative Journalism Today
  - Speaking Truth to Power

John Mair, Richard Lance Keeble and Farrukh Dhonday – Editors
- V.S. Naipaul:
  - The Legacy

Christian Wolmar
- Wolmar for London
  - Creating a Grassroots Campaign in a Digital Age

www.ingramcontent.com/pod-product-compliance
Lightning Source LLC
Chambersburg PA
CBHW052320220526
45472CB00001B/205